CAMBRIDGE GEOGRAPHICAL STUDIES

10 · WATER MANAGEMENT IN ENGLAND AND WALES

CAMBRIDGE GEOGRAPHICAL STUDIES

WATER MANAGEMENT IN ENGLAND AND WALES

ELIZABETH PORTER

CAMBRIDGE UNIVERSITY PRESS

CAMBRIDGE

LONDON · NEW YORK · MELBOURNE

Published by the Syndics of the Cambridge University Press
The Pitt Building, Trumpington Street, Cambridge CB2 1RP
Bentley House, 200 Euston Road, London NW1 2DB
32 East 57th Street, New York, NY 10022, USA
296 Beaconsfield Parade, Middle Park, Melbourne 3206, Australia

First published 1978

Printed in Malta by
Interprint (Malta) Ltd

SB 10495 [12 . 7.79

Library of Congress Cataloguing in Publication Data

Porter, Elizabeth.
Water management in England and Wales.

(Cambridge geographical studies; 10)
Bibliography: p.
Includes index.
1. Water-supply–England. 2. Water-supply–Wales. I. Title. II. Series.
TD57.P67   363,6'1'0942   77-83998
ISBN 0 521 21865 9

CONTENTS

FIGURES

ACKNOWLEDGEMENTS

The author wishes to thank the many people who helped during the book's preparation. These include staff of the Anglian, North West, Severn–Trent and Thames Water Authorities, the Central Water Planning Unit, the Department of the Environment Directorate of Water, the Flood Hazard Research Project at the Middlesex Polytechnic, the Institute of Hydrology, the Ministry of Agriculture, Fisheries and Food, the National Water Council and the Water Research Centre. I am especially indebted to Lord Ashby without whose initial encouragement the work might never have been undertaken, and to the Council of the Royal Society for a research grant from the 20th International Geographical Congress Fund.

The following kindly granted permission to reprint or modify material in figures and tables: Anglian Water Authority for figure 17 from *Eighth Annual Report 1972–3*, Great Ouse River Authority 1973; The Controller, Her Majesty's Stationery Office (Crown copyright reserved) for figures 11 and 27 and table 2 from *Water Resources in England and Wales* 1973, and for figures 14 and 15 from *Artificial Recharge of the London Basin: Hydrogeology* 1972; Institution of Civil Engineers for figure 18 from *Symposium on the Conservation of Water Resources in the United Kingdom* 1963; Institution of Water Engineers and Scientists for table 5 from *Water Treatment and Examination* **24** 1975; Methuen and Co Ltd for figure 4 from *Water, Earth and Man* 1969; Ministry of Agriculture, Fisheries and Food for figures 12 and 13 drawn from data collected in a special inquiry into irrigation 1975; North West Water Authority for figure 10 from *Ullswater/Windermere Scheme: Ullswater Works* Manchester Corporation Waterworks 1969 and for table 4 from *First Annual Report 1974–5*; Oxford University Press, Inc. for figure 22 from *Natural Hazards: Local, National, Global* by Gilbert F. White et al. Copyright © 1974 by Oxford University Press, Inc. Reprinted by permission; E. C. Penning-Rowsell and J. B. Chatterton for figures 23 and 24 from *The Benefits of Flood Alleviation: A Manual of Assessment Techniques* 1977; Severn–Trent Water Authority for figure 19 redrawn from a floodplain map by the Trent River Authority, for figure 21 from *Flood Forecasting and Flood Warning Procedure*, Trent River Authority 1970 and for figures 25 and 26 from *Water Quality 1973*; United States Army, Office of the Chief of Engineers for figure 20 from *Flood-Proofing Regulations* 1972.

CHAPTER 1

THE NATURE OF WATER MANAGEMENT

In 1969 a geographer could write: 'Perhaps the best tribute to the water supply industry in Britain has been the lack of interest which has been aroused in its activities. For most of us the supply of unlimited water of excellent quality at the turn of a tap has been taken for granted' (Jackson 1969: xiii). This lack of interest did not persist far into the 1970s. At the beginning of the decade a government advisory committee was devising a new management structure for the water industry, and the Water Act 1973, implemented the following year, wrought tremendous changes in the industry's organisation. Then came increases in the charges for water services, variable from place to place but many greatly in excess of general rates of inflation. Public alarm at the reorganisation and at the seemingly associated price rises led to a government review of the working of the 1973 Act and a promise of early amendment.

At the time of writing we are recovering from a severe drought. In August and September 1976 domestic supplies in south east Wales were cut off for part of the day and in areas of Devon the only water was from street standpipes. The government's legislative programme was rearranged to make room for an emergency Drought Act (August 1976), and the water industry, scarcely settled down after the upheavals of reorganisation, had to face the possibility that reservoirs and aquifers would not refill adequately during the winter. Relief has come with an unusually wet winter, but the memory of the drought is still vivid.

The drought was exceptional, unlike anything since rainfall records began in 1727, and it could be a mere aberration, although a serious disruption for agriculture, industry and domestic consumers of no lasting significance. More worrying is the suggestion that it may be evidence of a climatic change over Britain and north west Europe, which could give many years of lower rainfall. It is too early to know for sure. What is certain is that unlimited, cheap water supplies cannot be taken for granted.

But this book is not about crisis in the water industry, disturbing though the last few years have been. Rather it is about change in the water industry, and in particular the institutional and management changes that have helped the industry adapt itself to the task of giving the nation the water services it wants at costs it is prepared to pay. Indeed, it is thanks to recent changes that the worst drought for several centuries has not been a greater calamity. The drought has confirmed the success of many of the post-Water Act arrangements – and has emphasised certain deficiencies too. Further change is now inevitable.

Water management has been accepted as a public responsibility for a very long time. The ancient 'hydraulic civilisations' of Egypt, Babylonia, India and China depended on large scale engineering works for irrigation and flood prevention, and through the maintenance of the river works their governments were able to maintain a monopoly of social and political power. In the New World, pre-Columbian Peru and Mexico had elements of hydraulic civilisation, with strongly centralised government (Hall and Dracup 1970: 11; Smith 1969: 107–9). Britain never possessed a hydraulic civilisation in these terms – society was not organised around water management – but even here water management always seems to have had social and political dimensions.

It is obvious that the complexity of the water management problem increases when the demands for water services outstrip easily developable new resources. The first function of water management is the development of new resources, but when relatively low-cost possibilities have been exhausted and demand continues to rise, management has to assume a second function. This is the allocation of available resources among potential users, a 'rationing' of water services which may be effected by price, by administrative means or by a combination of the two. A third function, recycling, is necessary when new water is insufficient even with careful allocation. To some extent recycling occurs whenever sewage or other watery wastes are put into rivers upstream of abstraction points, but many modern water resource systems require recycling on a much greater scale than this. The regulation of effluent discharges and their integration with other water services becomes a major management task.

Our water management institutions have, over the years, taken upon themselves these three functions of development, allocation and recycling. The most recent changes, following the Water Act 1973, have been in the integration of effluent disposal. A decade earlier the Water Resources Act 1963 concentrated on water allocation.

This chapter goes on to explore the nature of the water management task, and especially those characteristics of the hydrologic system and of man's demands on it which determine the type of management needed. Following Craine's example in his study of the Water Resources Act 1963 (Craine 1969) and the water industry's deliberations both before and after the Water Act 1973 (Department of the Environment and Welsh Office 1970: 50–1; Central Advisory Water Committee 1971; Department of the Environment 1973a; Department of the Environment 1974a; Department of the Environment, Welsh Office, Ministry of Agriculture, Fisheries and Food 1976), we suggest institutional conditions which seem to favour good management.

Chapter 2 is a short review of the growth of water management legislation, emphasising the gradual convergence of responsibility for different water services upon the regional Water Authorities, and the problems of co-ordinating the work of regional units into a national water policy.

Then follows a series of case studies of different water services – public water supply, spray irrigation supply, flood damage reduction and effluent disposal. This is not intended to be a comprehensive list. Rather each service is chosen because it reveals a substantially different set of management problems. Present policies are shown in historical perspective, for most of the problems being tackled now with new weapons have been around for some years. Partial solutions have accumulated with time. Questions now are whether the management structure allows more complete solutions and whether it is flexible enough to tackle the different problems which are certain to be generated to replace those solved. As well as considering individual water services, we include a chapter on the contribution of groundwater to total resources, to complement the many references to sur-face sources and to draw out the special problems of controlling the exploita-tion of an invisible asset. Chapter 8 discusses aspects of water policy which transcend the boundaries of the regional Water Authorities and involve the whole nation. Finally we examine the water industry against the criteria of good management here set up.

The water management system

Water management can be considered as a man–environment system which transforms inputs of physical resources into desired outputs of water ser-vices. Man intervenes in the natural hydrologic system to increase the quantity of usable water and to modify its patterns of occurrence. However, man's control of the system is incomplete. Some inputs, rainfall for instance, are largely free of his influence; and some outputs, such as severe flood damage, are not what he desires.

Figure 1 illustrates this concept of water management. The management system at the centre of the figure uses structural and non-structural mea-sures, first to develop and modify inputs and then to allocate and recycle the transformed resources among the potential users to give the desired outputs of services. As well as being linked to each other via the manage-ment system, the inputs and outputs are themselves inter-linked. Reservoir and groundwater abstractions may be increased or decreased in order to regulate river flow; and river flow controls the replenishment of ground-water resources and of many surface reservoirs. The outputs of water ser-vices are inter-linked in that some can be had simultaneously and are thus complementary, such as recreation, amenity and navigation, while some are incompatible or conflicting, an increase in one resulting in a decrease in another. For example, if water is drawn out of a river for irrigation, a char-

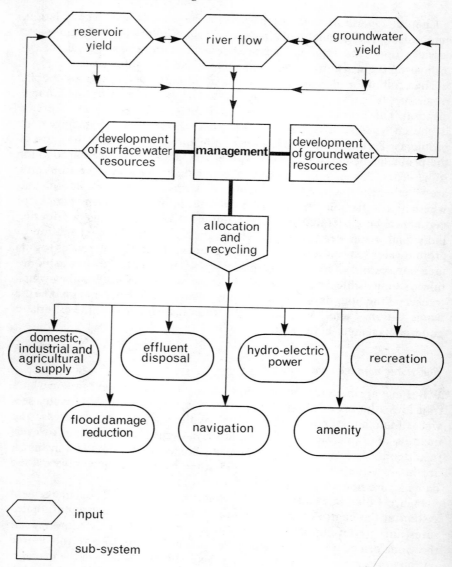

Figure 1   The water management system.

acteristically consumptive use, the river level may fall, restricting all those services with higher water level requirements. The central elements of the system, the water management techniques, are determined by the inputs and the desired outputs. They are there to create the one from the other.

System inputs – some characteristics of water resources

Figure 2 is a block diagram of a river basin, showing the main components of the basin hydrologic system. Figure 3 shows schematically the inter-relations of these same components. Precipitation in the form of rain, snow, hail or dew falls directly into river channels and bodies of standing water and also onto vegetation and the land surface below it. Some of this water evaporates or is transpired to the atmosphere, but much of that falling on the land is transferred over and through the soil to contribute to river flow or downwards to contribute to groundwater.

In the natural state, without the interference of man, evapotranspiration and river flow are the main outputs derived from precipitation, with water held in a number of storages or moving between them, *en route* through the system. These natural storages include the river channel, vegetation sur-faces and irregularities of the land surface retaining water usually only for a very short time, storage in the soil, and groundwater storage.

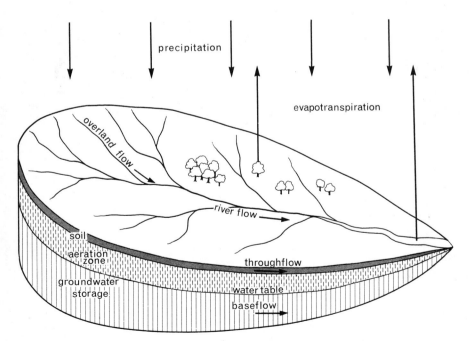

Figure 2   Block diagram of a river basin.

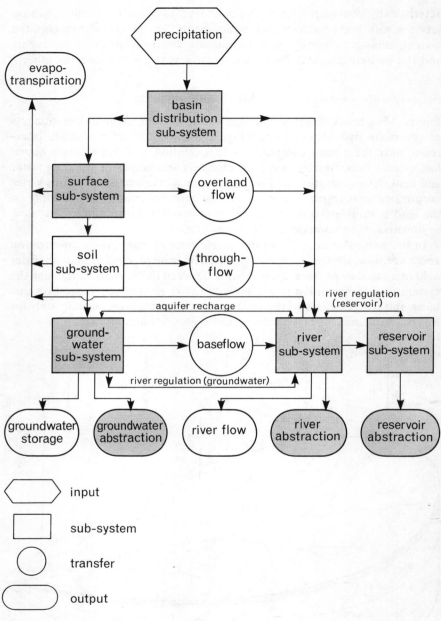

Figure 3   The river basin system: points of intervention.

Man's intervention in the hydrologic system has been concerned mainly with modifying the natural storages, although Chorley and More (1969: 157) have pointed out that no part has been entirely free of his experiments. Weather modification in general and induced precipitation and storm mitigation in particular could come to have an important influence in the future, but at present in Britain we may take the fundamental water input as given. Figure 3 shows, in the shaded sections, those points at which man has concentrated his efforts in water management.

By regulating the passage of water through the different storages, especially by diverting water from one to another and increasing the retention time in storage, man has gained partial control over his water resources. The first point of regulation is the basin distribution sub-system. Here incoming precipitation is divided between that going directly to river flow and that going through the various surface and soil storages. Alterations of the river network, drainage of wetlands or creation of new lakes and ponds will affect this division. The surface sub-system offers another opportunity to alter the amount of water going into the river, for instance by erosion control measures which reduce the overland flow of water during storms.

Some of the water percolating into the soil goes into groundwater storage in the aquifer where, under natural conditions, it contributes baseflow to the river when surface-derived flows are low and is itself recharged from the river when river levels are high. The hydrologic connection between groundwater and river flow has often been ignored by water engineers who have tended to treat the two sources quite separately. Traditionally the groundwater sub-system has been drawn upon for abstraction with little thought for the effects upon other groundwater users, let alone for the effects upon the river.

Direct abstraction from the river is the oldest form of water resource development, though it was soon found to be unsatisfactory because of natural fluctuations in flow. The off-stream storage of water in tanks, basins or reservoirs, to even out flow fluctuations, was a feature of the early hydraulic civilisations, and even today to many people water resource development means quite simply reservoir construction. Indeed it is arguable that the introduction of this extra, artificial storage element *is* the most influential of man's many interferences in the hydrologic system.

These traditional manipulations of the groundwater and river sub-systems give rise to three controlled outputs: groundwater abstraction, river abstraction and reservoir abstraction. Recently a greater understanding of the natural inter-relations between the components has led to more complex development measures, moving water to and fro between aquifer, river and reservoir. Of course these give the same type of outputs, but their interdependence and their efficiency are increased and more usable water is produced from the same physical resources.

Formerly, most of our reservoirs were used for direct supply, water being collected, stored and conveyed to consumers by pipe. The connection with the river was one way only: water was taken out of the river, or the head-waters were stopped off, and thereafter the water was distributed artificially, returning to the natural system again only as effluent after use. Recent changes in the operation of the same reservoirs gives a two way connection. Water is put into artificial storage as before, but in place of some of the direct, piped abstraction there are releases of water back to the river, to regulate flows for the benefit of river users. This is shown in figure 3 as 'river regulation'. A second form of river regulation is through controlled releases of groundwater into the river, to supplement its natural base-flow.

The final man-made connection between aquifer, river and reservoir sub-systems is the artificial recharge of the aquifer, when the aquifer is dewatered but there is surplus surface water. In effect this is the converse of ground-water abstraction for river regulation, water being taken from river (or reservoir) when supplies are in excess of demand and put into groundwater storage.

This outline of the hydrologic system shows two natural characteristics which have implications for good management. First is the flow character-istic of water. This gives opportunities for successive downstream uses of the same water, and also causes upstream abstractions or discharges to have downstream effects. No management system can afford to overlook this most basic feature. Second is the natural association of groundwater and river flow, which demands that the two types of source be managed with close reference to each other, even if fully integrated development is not possible.

A third resource characteristic not mentioned so far is the uneven spatial distribution of precipitation and of water-bearing rocks which gives an uneven distribution of physical resources. In England and Wales the areas of maximum precipitation are in the north and west, while the main aquifers underlie central and south east England. Groundwater is more important in the centre and south east, although it does not fully compensate for the region's deficiency in comparison with the rainier parts of the country. To compound the problem, it happens that some of the heaviest water demands are concentrated in areas of relatively meagre local resources.

The uneven distribution of water resources, together with the non-congruence of resource and demand patterns, means that some areas are not self-sufficient in water. They need to import it, perhaps from a few miles, perhaps from a hundred miles distant. This raises the question of appropriate size of the water management unit. If it is small there will be many transfers across its boundaries, involving negotiations with other units. As size in-creases the number of negotiated transfers decreases, but other management problems occur as local interest declines and centralised decision-making takes over. The ideal size of unit may be illusive, but the search for a practicable solution must take some account of the hydrologic base of resource distribution.

System outputs – the end products of water management

The desired results of water management may include water supplies for domestic, industrial and agricultural purposes, effluent disposal, reduction of flood damage, hydro-electric power, navigation, fisheries, recreation and amenity. To some extent what is desired is conditioned by what it is possible to attain. Hydro-electric power, an important product of water management in Canada and the United States, is ignored altogether in English water management, terrain and river flow precluding its development. In Scotland and to a lesser degree in Wales hydro-electric power *is* a possible and hence a desired output (Smith 1972: 145, 160).

In addition to the desired outputs there are those which come, whether desired or not, and reflect the incompleteness of man's control. Flood damage is in this category, a result of natural fluctuations in river flow. Then there are instances of man's intervention which have had unfortunate consequences. Water pollution comes to mind immediately. This is effluent disposal in excess, a reasonable use exaggerated until positive harm is done to other water services.

The various water services desired of the system are commonly classified in two ways. One classification separates those uses which take water out of the river (or aquifer) – abstractive uses – from those which utilise water *in situ* – in-channel uses. The difference is a fundamental one: in one case water is lost to the system, if only for a short time; in the other case it is always present. Abstractive uses include all domestic, industrial and agricultural supplies, and power station cooling. In-channel uses are sometimes further divided into flow and on-site uses (Sewell and Bower 1968: 12). Flow uses are those which require water to move in a designated channel, and among these are generation of hydro-electric power, reduction of flood damage, navigation and effluent disposal. On-site uses use water where it occurs naturally, the principal examples being wildlife and amenity.

The second classification separates consumptive from non-consumptive water uses, and to some extent it overlaps the abstractive/in-channel classification above. In the main, in-channel uses do not consume water, but nor are all abstractive uses consumptive. By consumptive we mean permanently lost to the system, that part of the abstraction that is not returned to the original or some other watercourse for reuse. Irrigation water evaporated, transpired and taken up by plant tissues is consumed in this sense, although of course the atmospheric water is eventually recycled as precipitation. Irrigation is a highly consumptive use, different authorities rating water loss at between 70 and 100 percent. On the other hand, consumption of water in domestic and industrial uses may be less than 10 percent, at least 90 percent being returned after use.

The water returned may, however, be sufficiently different from unused water to limit its further utility. Deterioration in quality and increases in temperature are very common. Both may adversely affect wildlife and, while increases in temperature do not usually in themselves bother abstractors other than those hoping to use the water for cooling purposes, quality deterioration can impose such additional costs on potential users that reuse is restricted or even abandoned. Temperature has an influence on water quality, affecting the amount of dissolved oxygen held in the water. Dissolved oxygen is an indicator of good water quality, and dissolved oxygen concentrations decrease as temperature increases. Temperature and quality must therefore be considered together as limits on water reuse.

This serves to amplify the idea that some water uses are complementary while others are conflicting. Figure 4 shows the links between different water uses. The in-channel uses (flood damage reduction, hydro-electric power, effluent disposal and recreation) are largely complementary, although complementarity or conflict between effluent disposal and recreation depends on water quality. In general the abstractive and consumptive uses (irrigation, domestic and industrial water supplies) are in conflict with in-channel uses. An exception is flood damage reduction. This often requires a degree of regulation of river flow by reservoir storage and so is rendered complementary to water supply which also benefits from river regulation.

Here we need to define more closely the concept of multiple use of the water resource. It has two distinct aspects, one the reuse potential of any given unit of water and the other the several purposes that water control structures may serve. Each has implications for water management. The reuse potential, so easily reduced by consumptive abstraction and quality deterioration, forces upon management a concern for resource allocation and recycling. An appropriation of water by highly consumptive or polluting uses will certainly restrict its use for other purposes, and it is a management task to decide if such an appropriation is justified. Maximum diversity of use is not necessarily the correct answer.

The second aspect of multiple use is the multi-purpose potential of water control structures, particularly reservoirs. The English and Welsh reservoirs now operated partly for river regulation act to hold back flood flows, augment low summer flows, give direct supplies to consumers and provide recreation opportunities. Not surprisingly there are both complementarities and conflicts here, in initial design and in operating procedures. An example that can be observed nearly every year is the late summer drawdown of the reservoirs resulting from direct abstraction and river regulation releases. This creates storage for anticipated high winter runoff but inconveniences those using the reservoir for recreation. Again management is involved in

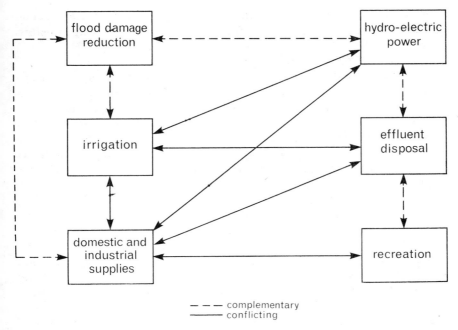

— — — complementary
——— conflicting

Figure 4   Complementary and conflicting water uses.
Based on O'Riordan and More 1969:550.

deciding the purposes to be served and the priorities in serving them, when the maximum amounts of each cannot be had simultaneously.

The centre of the system – management techniques

From a consideration of system inputs and outputs – water resources and the demands for water services – we turn to the management techniques which transform inputs to outputs. By now it is clear that some of the system's elements are so inter-meshed that this simple transformation model must not be over-worked. In all but the least developed regions of the world some of the inputs have already been acted upon by man, and in this country the pattern of water resources is far from natural. Modern water management systems will find both their inputs and their outputs partly predetermined, inputs by existing reservoirs and well fields, desired outputs by existing patterns of land use in the river basin.

Enlarging on the management system of figure 1 (p. 4), we may define management techniques as follows:

1 the development of water resources,
2 the allocation of resources among potential users, and
3 the recycling of water to facilitate reuse.

All three assume an adequate information service, providing factual data about current supplies and demands, projections for the future and identification of alternative ways of meeting future demands. We may therefore define another technique:

4 water management information.

The development of water resources is effected mainly through construction work, although the operation of former direct supply reservoirs in a river regulating mode gives certain limited opportunities for increasing water resources without investment in new works. Construction work is necessary again for water recycling, and chapter 7 shows there is heavy expenditure just now to modernise and extend the sewage treatment plants which the Water Authorities inherited with the reorganisation of water services.

Development of new resources and recycling of used water together yield the water to be allocated among potential users (although allocation and recycling often present a typical chicken-and-egg problem of antecedence). The oldest means of effecting an allocation is by water rights under the common law. In England riparian owners have a right to the water that flows through or past their property, undiminished in quantity or quality by the actions of upstream users. Obviously this right is based on assumptions of non-consumptive and non-polluting use and as a result has only the most limited practical application. The eastern, more humid part of the United States adopted the same riparian principle, while in the west there are appropriative rights, 'first in time, first in right'.

Statute law generates other water rights and obligations. From the first half of the nineteenth century several major pieces of English legislation attempted to meet recognised deficiencies in the common law, but only in the last thirty years or so has the administrative machinery been built up to enforce these rights and obligations. Licensing control, instituted for certain groundwater abstractions in 1945, for effluent disposal in 1951 and for river abstractions in 1963, is the established method of regulating water use, dividing the resource between different categories of user and fixing standards of quality for returned water.

A less used method of regulating water use is the pricing of water services so as to influence demand. Chapter 4 discusses allocation and charging policies in relation to water supply for spray irrigation, and present evidence suggests that charges for abstracted water are not in themselves the major curb on demand. However, there is a growing interest in devising charging schemes for abstracted and returned water which reflect more closely the real costs imposed on the system and so encourage individual consumers to use water services more efficiently (Department of the Environment and Welsh Office 1970: 44; Royal Commission on Environmental Pollution 1972: 74–85; Department of the Environment 1973b, 1974b).

It is no easy matter to determine the correct price or value of water services. They are essentially natural monopolies, and there is no market in which to establish competitive prices. Water is usually considered as a 'free good', and the charges imposed are for source development, treatment, distribution and disposal, not for water *per se*. It is the broad objective of the charging schemes being formulated now to set charges to reflect marginal costs of development, treatment and so on, when all spillover or social costs are included.

We have already noted that the hydrologic system causes upstream actions to have downstream effects and that ground and surface waters are inter-linked. These physical characteristics have social and economic con-sequences which are often ignored by individual water users operating in isolation but which have to be acknowledged on a larger scale. Spillover or social costs and benefits can be apportioned to users throughout the manage-ment unit, even if their individual operations are usually costed without them.

The efficacy of each of these management techniques depends on ade-quate information. Hydrologic information is the obvious starting point, and government agencies have been involved in data collection, analysis and dissemination since 1935 when the Ministry of Health set up the Inland Water Survey. Collection of specific social and economic data followed later, although population census materials have long been used for pre-diction of water supply and effluent disposal demands. Monitoring studies of the effects upon demand of different licensing and charging policies are especially important today, as water availability and cost invalidate simple extrapolations of past demand trends. The necessary data base is expanding from factual, mainly hydrologic information to include more equivocal information about the likely effects of alternative management policies.

Decision-making in water management

The consideration of alternative policies raises questions about the decision process. There are two opposing, extreme models of the decision process, one an ideal of rationality, the other a depressing description of administra-tive reality.

The ideal model of how decisions ought to be made stresses man's rationality as an economic being. Decision-making involves:

1 identification of the value or values to be maximised,
2 ranking of values in terms of relative importance when values conflict,
3 identification of alternative possible courses of action,
4 determination of the consequences that follow from each alternative, and
5 comparative evaluation of the consequences of the alternatives in terms of the value or values to be maximised.

The real world model on the other hand admits that the identification of values and their ranking are difficult. Lack of time and resources cuts short the search for alternatives, some of which are in any case impossible candidates because of prevailing law or vested interest. The range of possibilities is so narrowed that the alternatives compared differ only very slightly from each other. Such successive limited comparisons, as Lindblom (1959) termed them, confine new policies to a band on the periphery of former policy, even when a policy entirely unrelated to the old may be the only workable one (Marshall 1964). Between the two extremes come Simon's notions of bounded rationality, with choice limited by the perception of feasible alternatives, and a search for reasonably adequate, not necessarily optimal solutions (Simon 1960, 1967).

There is a special problem in the complex scientific foundation of many water management decisions. While the water engineer is uniquely able to understand this, he is not specially equipped to judge the values and costs of the various water services to the people affected. Fox (1966) asked the questions, can those affected by management decisions use the scientific evidence well enough to arrive at intelligent positions of their own, or must they leave to the water engineer the responsibility for value judgements on their behalf.

We must also consider the ultimate purpose of water management. O'Riordan (1971: 110–14) showed the possible diversity of goals. So far we have by-passed the issue by assuming that the goal is to produce desired outputs of water services, but this is open to two different interpretations.

The more customary one is that the government has a responsibility to provide the water services demanded by the community, a responsibility to plan to meet the requirements of the predicted population. If the demand exists, it must be met. Only recently have we seen this principle tempered by a policy suggestion that it is desirable to provide water services only when their value to the user is greater than their cost to the community (Department of the Environment 1973b: 8). Forms of cost–benefit analysis have been used for some years in judging the worthwhileness of flood protection schemes, but other water services have not been subject to similar economic appraisal.

Even the qualification that benefits should exceed costs does not move one far towards the goal of economic efficiency. In contrast, the second interpretation of the purpose of water management takes this as its base – the allocation of existing resources to the highest possible economic use. It operates in two spheres, one *within* water management, for the allocation of water to the highest yielding uses, and the other *between* water management and other public sector investments, for the allocation of public funds to the highest yielding enterprises. It has been suggested that 'all investments in the water services must . . . be weighed carefully against competing claims within the public sector' (Department of the Environment 1973b: 5), but the present decision-making structure does not facilitate any formal economic comparison.

Some criteria for judging a water management system

The water management system established by the Water Act 1973 was the subject of government review within the space of two years, an acknowledgement that institutional arrangements really matter in water management and that they are not easy to perfect in a single reorganisation. One of the principal pressures for review was that water services suddenly seemed to have become much more expensive. Where water charges increased far above the general rate of inflation simultaneously with reorganisation, it was natural to assume that one caused the other and that both were wrong. But by what criteria is a water management system to be judged? None are predetermined, but in developing our own we are assisted by the earlier definition of the management system's inputs, outputs and internal management techniques.

Does the system allow integrated management of all aspects of water use? Two main arguments have been put forward for preserving the unity of the basin hydrologic system. First the flow characteristic of water gives the possibility of successive reuse but also tends to dissociate cause and effect, cost and benefit along the length of the river. Both are best accommodated by managing the river as one entity. Secondly the natural links between flowing water and water in storage require the management of water not just in the river but in and between storages as well.

These hydrologic considerations have territorial and functional implications for the management unit. The management unit must deal with one or a group of river basins (the problem of size is discussed below) and it must be effective in all terrestrial aspects of the water cycle – collection, storage, distribution, abstraction, return and reuse.

Can the management unit apply the full range of management techniques? This criterion is a close parallel to that of Craine (1969: 20) and asks, can the management unit apply the techniques of resource development, allocation and recycling, based on adequate information? Are the techniques available through legal authorisation to undertake these activities, and are the authorised activities under unified control? Only if all the techniques are available can the management unit fulfil its integrating task above.

Is the size of the unit such as to accommodate hydrologic interdependencies and to effect economies of scale? The uneven spatial distribution of water resources means that some trading between management units is necessary, unless the unit comprises the whole country. The smaller the unit the less likely it is to have control over the sources supplying its centres of demand, and the more inter-unit transfers there will have to be. Physical transfers of water require financial transfers too, to compensate for the hydrologic interdependency effects just given as the justification for unity of management. The smaller the management unit the less chance there is of the natural accommodation of hydrologic links.

Size of unit, in territory and financial resources, controls the scale of works for water development and treatment. Economies to be had through large scale construction come about only if units are themselves large or if effective combinations of units can be formed. Only a management unit covering England and Wales together will remove completely the need for inter-unit transfers and joint construction schemes. Anything smaller must face problems of shared responsibility.

Does the system encourage efficiency in water use and in public investment? Efficiency in water use requires the reduction of losses and waste and the allocation of water services to those consumers who most value them. 'Value' may be expressed solely in terms of the prices consumers are prepared to pay for services, or may incorporate non-monetary social values as well. Efficiency in public investment refers to the balance between investment in water services and investment in other sectors of the economy. Again the requirement is that investment goes where it is most valued. Water services and public funds are both scarce: hence the concern with economic issues. Not everyone can be served fully, simultaneously and continuously. Allocation decisions are inevitable. This criterion asks, in effect, are the allocation decisions made in a way conducive to efficiency?

Efficient use of resources can be encouraged by giving consumers price incentives to adjust their demands for water services. The charging policies developed by the Water Authorities are of fundamental importance here and they must be examined with this criterion in mind. Some public values associated with water services may not be directly expressed in prices to individual consumers, and if so one must inquire how these values are taken into account in allocation decisions and what effects they have on efficiency.

Can all relevant interests contribute to water management decisions? In one respect at least this is an extension of the question above. Many, though not necessarily all, interests in water management have an economic expression. This criterion is broader, however, and its significance increases as the likelihood of an affirmative answer to the efficiency question decreases. If the system does not work automatically towards an efficient allocation of resources, the processes of administrative allocation become more important.

The main impact of water policy decisions is felt locally, both in benefit and in cost, and the consideration of local interests, the points of view of all categories of consumers, is thus a first requirement. Another requirement is that the scientific basis of water policy should be well understood at management level, and this is not necessarily met through representation of local beneficiary and cost bearer interests. Affected interests extend beyond those of consumers of water services. Landowners and countryside and wildlife groups have interests in water developments, especially those involving the drowning of land or the lowering of the water table, and these interests too must be incorporated in water policy decisions.

Are there effective links between management units, with national bodies and with central government? A decentralised management system founded on river basin units must face the problem that not all management issues can be dealt with internally. For inter-unit water transfers or joint construction works to occur, there must be good working relations between the units, both between pairs of units and among them all together. Then some of the units' research needs in hydrology and economic and engineering aspects of water management may be better met by work at national, not regional level. The co-ordination of investment in water services with investment in other public sectors is a matter for the central government, which also has a concern to see that the operations of the individual management units do not diverge from each other so much that they upset public confidence.

One must ask how effective is the cooperation between the regional management units and the national organisations, and how can national water policies (if such are desired) be implemented through a system the principal units of which are regional and autonomous.

WATER MANAGEMENT LEGISLATION IN ENGLAND AND WALES

The Water Act 1973 which came into effect on 1 April 1974 and underlies the present management system builds upon a body of water law and practice developed gradually over the last century. While there is no need to review this in its entirety, it is interesting to trace the origins of certain modern features, particularly the evolution of the regional management unit and its current management techniques.

First, however, a word is needed about the larger territorial unit, England and Wales. The Water Act 1973 and its predecessors all refer to England and Wales and exclude Scotland and Northern Ireland, neither of which has directly equivalent legislation. Smith, completing *Water in Britain* at a Scottish university, acknowledged a case for extending the legislative framework over the whole of the United Kingdom (Smith 1972: 34–5), but the fact remains that England and Wales are a natural hydrologic unit, sharing the Severn, the Dee and the Wye river systems, while the main water resources of Scotland are separated from those of northern England by the divide of the Cheviots. If management is to be based on river basins, England and Wales must be considered together. The inclusion of Scotland is less necessary on hydrologic grounds.

It is a fundamental premise of the present system that the appropriate unit of management *is* the river basin or a grouping of river basins, for the reasons outlined in chapter 1. The idea was current in the 1870s, but it did not become effective over the whole country until the River Boards Act 1948. Another idea of longstanding is that of comprehensive management, all aspects of water development, distribution, return and reuse coming under the control of one authority, and the 1973 Act pursues comprehensive management much farther than did earlier legislation.

Around the middle of the last century both these ideas were encompassed in the term 'rivers conservancy'. The Duke of Richmond introduced a Bill with that title into Parliament in 1878, and the Council of the Society of Arts offered to give medals for useful suggestions for dividing England and Wales into watershed districts suitable for conservancy purposes. The essay of Frederick Toplis, awarded a Silver Medal, advocated a system strikingly similar in its territorial units and management powers to that adopted almost a century later (Toplis 1879). It is even a little disconcerting to compare his map of proposed watershed districts with that of the present Water Authorities (figures 5 and 6). Differences there are, of course, particularly in the Welsh Borders, but the similarities are more remarkable. No such similarities were to be found between Toplis' districts and those of the other five essayists whose suggestions were published alongside his, no doubt one factor operating against an early division of the country into river basin units.

Toplis proposed that each of his river basin units be managed by a body of commissioners, supported by competent legal and engineering advisers and with powers to acquire all existing waterworks and to manage them together with the rivers in the interests of water supply, pollution prevention and flood prevention. In effect 'every drop of water falling on their district should be more or less under their control from the time it falls on the land until it reaches the sea' (Toplis 1879: 698). Only in the last few years has this become a reality.

A proper explanation of the delay is beyond the scope of this study, but we will trace the evolution of the present Water Authorities and their gradual accumulation of the powers recognised as 'absolutely necessary' in 1879. The convergence of responsibility upon the regional management unit is shown especially clearly in three main strands of water management: land drainage and flood prevention; water supply; and pollution prevention (see figure 7).

Land drainage and flood prevention

This has a particularly long legal history. In the thirteenth century the Lords, Bailiff and Jurats of Romney Marsh were involved in wetland drainage to improve agriculture (Johnson 1966: 29), and Commissioners of Sewers were established in 1427 and 1531 to protect land from inundation (Wisdom 1962: 29). Perhaps as a result of early and widespread local provisions, the modern drainage law crystallised comparatively early, in 1930. While other aspects of water management have undergone great upheavals in the last few decades, land drainage and flood prevention continue to this day on the 1930s model.

The Land Drainage Act 1930 has a significance beyond land drainage and flood prevention. It set up Catchment Boards, each covering a major river basin or group of smaller rivers, and endowed with general powers for land drainage in the catchment and special powers for flood prevention on certain defined 'main' rivers. After 1948 the Catchment Boards gave way to River Boards which had additional responsibilities for fisheries, pollution prevention and river gauging and now covered the whole country. The River Boards in turn were replaced by River Authorities and then by Water

Figure 5   Watershed districts proposed by Frederick Toplis in 1879
Source: Toplis 1879:697.

Figure 6   Water Authorities in England and Wales.

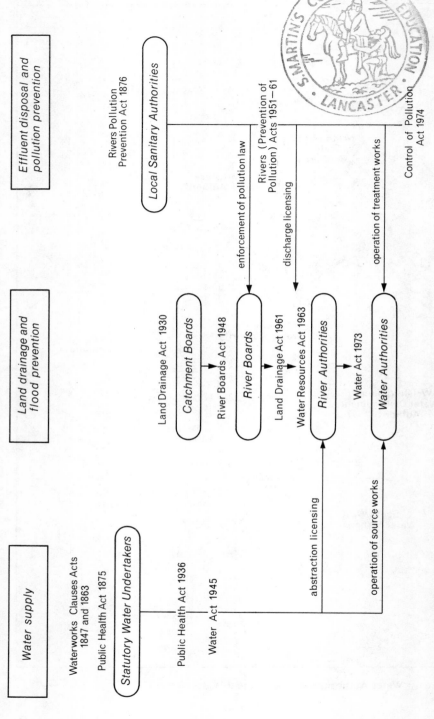

Figure 7 Convergence of responsibility for water services upon the Water Authorities.

Authorities, each assuming further water management powers. In the Catchment Boards, solely for land drainage and flood prevention, we find the original regional units of water management.*

The Catchment Boards set up Internal Drainage Boards in those areas where land would derive special benefit from drainage, and got their operating funds from precepts on these Boards and on the County and County Borough Councils in their catchments. In addition the central government gave grants for approved work. Today grant-aid from the Ministry of Agriculture, Fisheries and Food towards engineering work for land drainage and flood prevention is the only government subsidy the Water Authorities receive. All other water services have to be self-financing.

Not all flood problems are best tackled by engineering works, of course, and in 1947, at the suggestion of the Ministry of Town and Country Planning, town planners and the Catchment Boards began to cooperate to prevent new or extended building in flood hazard areas. A more recent addition to the water agencies'** responsibilities is flood forecasting, based on the hydrometric networks which the River Authorities installed or improved after the Water Resources Act 1963.

The Water Act 1973, revolutionary in respect of water supply and effluent disposal, left the arrangements for land drainage and flood prevention virtually unaltered. The powers to finance and construct works, given in the Land Drainage Acts of 1930 and 1961 have been amended only slightly by the Water Act 1973 and the Land Drainage (Amendment) Act 1976, providing one of the few examples of continuity in the otherwise rapidly changing organisation of water management.

Water supply

Though several types of abstractive demand for water are distinguishable – domestic supply, industrial supply, water for farm animals, for irrigation and so on – government concern for water supply began with domestic supply and was limited to this until the Water Act 1945. The provision of water was originally a sanitary, public health service. The growing urban populations of the early nineteenth century were, in the fortunate areas, supplied with water by new organisations, private companies or local public authorities deriving their powers direct from Parliament by local Acts. At first there was little uniformity in the operating rules of these, the statutory water undertakers, but the Waterworks Clauses Acts of 1847 and 1863 gave

*The Conservators of the River Thames (established by local Act in 1857) and the Lee Conservancy Board (local Act 1868) are exceptions to this general statement. Both discharged a range of water management functions, and both have now been absorbed into the Thames Water Authority.

**The term 'water agency' is non-specific and is used for any water management organisation – statutory water undertaker, Catchment Board, River Board, River Authority or Water Authority.

models for them to incorporate in their own legislation. Public Health Acts in 1875 and 1936 set out the basic code for domestic water supply.

The statutory water undertakers were obliged by the terms of their establishment to provide water for domestic purposes, and increasing demand forced them to carry out more and more source development, often at a distance from the consuming area. When local supplies ran out or became polluted, the undertakers looked to remote, undeveloped upland areas where they soon found themselves in conflict, both with local interests and with other water undertakers with similar ideas. Each new source development needed a Parliamentary Act. Parliamentary Committees considered the individual Bills submitted, but they had no continuing existence and no responsibility to consider the regional allocation of water resources. Each development scheme was judged in isolation by an *ad hoc* Committee.

Rivalries between water undertakers suggested that what was needed was some form of regional planning for water supply. In 1869 the Royal Commission on Water Supply, under the Duke of Richmond, had advocated regional planning, and the suggestion was revived several times over the next fifty years. In 1920 the Water Power Resources Committee (Board of Trade) proposed a central Water Commission for England and Wales, empowered to establish regional watershed boards. The Water Commission did not materialise, but from 1924 there was some slight movement forwards when the water undertakers and the Ministry of Health set up Regional Advisory Water Committees to coordinate undertakers' efforts in joint schemes for water supply.

The Water Act 1945 greatly increased the central government's involvement with water supply problems and supervision of the water undertakers, and marks the beginning of a national water supply policy. The Act also broadened the basis of the water supply function, requiring water undertakers to supply water for non-domestic as well as domestic purposes. Another feature, small in itself but which has grown to be an important element of present policy, was the control of new groundwater abstractions in designated conservation areas. This was the beginning of abstraction licensing.

In the early 1940s, when the Central Advisory Water Committee (under Lord Milne) was examining the structure of water management, there was an opportunity to bring water supply together with other aspects of water use in a comprehensive management system centred on the river basin. The Milne Committee preferred instead a separation between the powers of the new river basin organisations it was advocating – the River Boards – and those of the existing statutory water undertakers (Central Advisory Water Committee 1943). Thus the River Boards Act 1948 had little effect on the water supply industry. The River Boards took over general responsibility for the conservation of water resources in their areas, and had specific authority to collect information about water abstractions and returns to the river system, but they had no control over the activities of the water undertakers. In particular the undertakers could appropriate and develop new sources of supply without reference to the River Boards.

The Water Resources Act 1963 also stopped short of full integration of water supply with other aspects of water management, although through its system of licences and charges for all water abstractions it provided a means of allocating water among potential users. No water undertaker could now abstract from a source except under licence from the River Authority, and the River Authority had overall control of the development of new source works.

Nevertheless, most existing source works remained the property of the water undertakers. In 1971 the Central Advisory Water Committee (under Sir Alan Wilson) found the resulting inflexibility in the use of reservoirs and supply lines a serious defect in the organisation of water supply, and the Water Act 1973, partly based on the Wilson Committee's findings, tackled the problem by ending the independent life of the statutory water undertakers. In April 1974 the Water Authorities took over the functions and assets of all local authority water undertakings, only some thirty water companies remaining as separate organisations operating under agency agreements with the Water Authorities. Thus only recently has the regional unit of water management taken the main responsibility for water supply, and its direct control will not be complete until the water companies are taken into the Water Authorities.

Effluent disposal and the prevention of pollution

Before the Industrial Revolution most of Britain's rivers were free of serious pollution: self-purification processes dealt fairly adequately with the effluent load. Yet as early as 1388 statute law had recognised water pollution as an offence. A statute of Richard II prohibited the throwing of dung, filth and garbage into ditches and rivers near cities and towns, and statutes of Henry VIII and George II sought to protect navigable waters from the deposition of solid wastes (Wisdom 1966: 7–8).

Throughout the nineteenth century there was a progressive deterioration in river quality, due first to a quite sudden rise in industrial pollution and then, from mid century onwards, to the addition of increasing volumes of domestic sewage from the towns' new and expanding waterborne sewerage systems.* In 1808 Manchester's River Irwell was described as 'black as ink' (quoted in Briggs 1968: 89), and indeed across the Pennines the water of the Yorkshire Calder was used as ink by an angry manufacturer writing to the Royal Commission on Rivers Pollution in 1869. The writer appended 'Could

---

*Waterborne sewerage systems were first introduced about 1810, but until mid century they were uncommon.

the odour only accompany this sheet, it would add much to the interest of this memorandum!' (quoted in Klein 1957: 4) In London in the summers of 1858 and 1859 the stench of the River Thames was so foul with sewage that 'the atmosphere of Parliamentary Committee rooms was only rendered barely tolerable by the suspension before every window of blinds saturated with chloride of lime, and by the lavish use of this and other disinfectants' (Dr William Budd, quoted in Klein 1957: 3). Cholera epidemics in London and the northern manufacturing towns in the 1860s and 1870s drew attention to the physical as well as the aesthetic evils of polluted rivers, and at last in 1876 comprehensive legislation was introduced which, it was hoped, would effectively combat pollution.

The Rivers Pollution Prevention Act 1876 was the basic water pollution law for three quarters of a century, but this long appearance in the statute book does not signify success. From its enactment it suffered from two factors militating against strong control of pollution: the safeguards and reservations it contained to protect industrial interests; and the multiplicity of authorities charged with its administration. It was not an offence if a discharger could show he had used the best practical and available means to render the effluent harmless. Even if he had not done his best here, no action could be taken against him that would materially injure his enterprise. The responsibility for the whole length of a river from source to mouth was often divided between dozens of urban and rural sanitary authorities, making coordinated control impossible. The sewers of the sanitary authorities were themselves major polluters, because of a general reluctance to spend money on treatment works for the benefit of other water users downstream. Setting such a poor example, the sanitary authorities could hardly take strong action against industrial polluters. Thrift and the desire to expand industrial production prevailed over considerations of river quality, and in spite of the 1876 Act river pollution worsened in many areas.

In a few areas the problems of fragmented responsibility were solved by the creation of Conservancy or Rivers Boards. The Thames and Lee Conservancy Boards pre-dated the 1876 Act which they then administered in their catchments, and in the 1890s four Rivers Boards were set up for some of the more seriously polluted rivers in northern England. Elsewhere more coordinated efforts for pollution prevention had to wait until the River Boards Act 1948.

The water pollution law was itself completely overhauled in 1951. The 1876 Act was prohibitive: no polluting substances, whether sewage, manufacturing effluent or mine water, were to be discharged. Absolute prohibition was obviously impossible – hence the disabling qualifications in respect of industry. The 1951 Rivers (Prevention of Pollution) Act abandoned prohibition for a quite different system of discharge licensing, the River Boards consenting to and controlling new discharges by prescribing standards for quality and quantity. The system has since been extended, by the Rivers

(Prevention of Pollution) Act 1961 and Part II of the Control of Pollution Act 1974, to cover all discharges, new and old, to both non-tidal and tidal rivers and estuaries, and today the consent conditions imposed on the discharger are the principal weapons against water pollution.

Until 1948 the enforcement of the pollution law was the job of the local sanitary authorities whose sewers were in very many areas contributing the largest of all polluting loads. This 'fundamental mistake' (Smith 1972:25) has repercussions to this day. Such an arrangement did nothing to encourage early investment in sewage treatment works, and although the Rivers (Prevention of Pollution) Acts 1951 and 1961, administered by independent organisations, spurred the local authorities to greater efforts and greater investment, the Working Party on Sewage Disposal (Department of the Environment and Welsh Office 1970: 9) suggested that over 3000 sewage plants were producing effluents inferior to what could reasonably be expected from modern treatment methods.

The Water Act 1973 provided a radical solution. Responsibility for sewage treatment and disposal was taken away from the local authorities, almost a century after their first involvement, and placed with the new Water Authorities. Nearly 1400 separate sewage authorities were collapsed into ten regional units. This not only enlarged the financial basis for sewage disposal and aided regional rationalisation of treatment works, it at last recognised sewage disposal as part of the total hydrologic system, as a major recycling element in water management. Separatism and excessive fragmentation of responsibility came to an end and were immediately replaced by problems of coordinating regional management of existing works and of generating capital for necessary investment, so long delayed.

The Water Act 1973 and the Water Authorities

The Water Resources Act 1963 was declared 'a water management charter', 'a giant step forward in England's response to contemporary water problems' (Craine 1969: 42, 120), 'an entirely new approach to water problems' (Smith 1972: 34), and one is inclined to apply the same comments, *a fortiori*, to the 1973 legislation. But there is always a temptation to assume that the most recent enactment is the successful culmination of all earlier legislative attempts. The 1963 Act's River Authorities survived for only ten years, and this should caution us against the automatic assumption that the 1973 Act contains the final word on the subject of water management.

Indeed, only two months after the implementation of the Water Act 1973, the Department of the Environment announced that the working of the Act would be reviewed (June 1974). The resulting consultative document *Review of the Water Industry in England and Wales* was published early in 1976 (Department of the Environment, Welsh Office and Ministry of Agriculture, Fisheries and Food 1976), and modifications of the charging system are incorporated in the Water Charges Equalisation Act 1977. Further changes are probable in the near future, but these will not be revolutionary. The water industry might not survive a second major reorganisation within such a short time, but the *Review* emphasises, if emphasis is needed, the industry's essential dynamism.

The Water Act 1973 established ten Water Authorities, nine in England and one in Wales – the Welsh National Water Development Authority. Figure 7 (p. 22) illustrates how the new authorities have developed from organisations which had as their initial concern only land drainage and flood prevention. Over the years other functions were added, first those to do with flowing water, principally pollution prevention and fisheries, and then functions to do with abstraction. The latest addition is responsibility for water supply, sewerage and sewage disposal.

A corollary of the extended functions of the Water Authorities is the disappearance of other organisations formerly concerned with water management. The local authorities have lost, or been relieved of, all their functions in respect of water supply; 157 local authority or joint board water undertakings disappeared in the reorganisation. The local authorities are still responsible for local sewerage systems – the smaller sewage pipes – but main sewers and all treatment plants and outfalls have passed into Water Authority control. The twenty-nine River Authorities have of course disappeared as well, and their ten successors have taken on the work of around 1580 former units, a phenomenal reduction in numbers.

It is difficult to exaggerate the magnitude of the change. Three main groups of water interests – river management, water supply and sewage disposal – come together for the first time, with a simultaneous increase in the territory covered by each management unit. The reorganisation was preceded by a detailed study of appropriate forms of management. The Management Structure Committee, appointed by the Secretary of State for the Environment in 1972, proposed a two-tier organisation for the Water Authorities, regional headquarters delegating responsibility to smaller divisional units (Department of the Environment 1973a: 11). For the first few years at least it was suggested that the divisions be based on former River Authorities as rivers divisions, statutory water undertakers as water supply divisions, and newly formed divisions for sewage disposal. The new Authorities took this advice and retained the outline of the old system until they felt able to adopt fully integrated management at divisional level. The Severn–Trent Water Authority was the first to make the second-phase change in management.

National water policy and institutions

The *Review of the Water Industry in England and Wales* endorsed the catchment-based Water Authority as the most appropriate unit for regional management but proposed substantial changes to the national water institutions. There is a continuing search for an effective organisation at national level, for over the last fifteen years views have changed and changed again about the desirability of a strong national organisation and about the proper balance of power between central government and independent water institutions.

The first explicit attempts to frame a national water policy were in the Water Act 1945. This gave the Minister of Housing and Local Government the responsibility 'to promote the conservation and proper use of water resources and the provision of water supplies in England and Wales and to secure the effective execution by water undertakers, under his control and direction, of a national policy relating to water'. But one may ask what is the purpose of a national policy for water, if it is assumed that local or regional management units are doing their jobs reasonably well? The 1945 Act specified two Ministerial functions. One was the conservation of water for supply, mainly through the licensing of certain groundwater abstractions and the prevention of pollution of sources drawn upon for supply. Later on these types of control were transferred to the regional management units. The other function was the supervision of the statutory water undertakers, particularly the rationalisation of their service areas, and this, the coordination of individual units' operations, has remained a national concern.

Though the term 'national policy' appeared in the legislation, there was little done to effect it, beyond the amalgamation of certain water undertakers, until a central authority was set up to promote an active programme for the whole country. The Water Resources Board, established in 1964 under the Water Resources Act, was such an authority, a national agency for data collection, research and planning, and independent of central government. Among its responsibilities was the coordination of local and regional water management schemes with inter-regional and national needs. Its three major studies of regional water resources (Water Resources Board 1966a, 1970, 1971) led the Board to conclude that substantial inter-river transfers were needed, within the three regions (the North, the South East, and Wales and the Midlands) and even between them. The Board's report *Water Resources in England and Wales* (1973a)* outlined alternative national strategies for meeting the demands for water to the beginning of the next century.

The Water Resources Board was an advisory body, with no powers to compel individual River Authorities to cooperate together and no powers to construct and operate schemes except for research purposes. It wielded its influence, which was very considerable in some instances, entirely through negotiation, but a case was strongly argued that in the reorganised water industry the Board's successor should have executive responsibility through

*Dated 1973, in fact published early in 1974.

reserve powers to undertake major projects (Central Advisory Water Committee 1971: 71–3).

Instead the Water Resources Board disappeared altogether, and there was no direct successor. The reorganisation weakened the national organisation outside central government, strengthened the involvement of the Department of the Environment, and divided the functions of data collection, research and planning between new agencies.

The Water Act 1973 established as national water institutions the National Water Council and the Water Space Amenity Commission. The Water Space Amenity Commission was an entirely new creation, to foster better relations between water interests and those of recreation and amenity. The National Water Council was the national consultative and advisory body for the water services, like the Water Resources Board reporting in two directions, to the regional management units and to central government, but with its research and planning functions much reduced from those of the Board.

At the Board's demise, the Department of the Environment took on the additional functions of data collection and national planning, and set up the Water Data Unit and the Central Water Planning Unit to assist the Secretary of State in these new areas.

The reorganisation also produced a new central research organisation, the Water Research Centre, amalgamating the Water Pollution Research Laboratory, the Water Research Association and parts of the Technology Division of the Water Resources Board. The Water Research Centre retained the voluntary membership form of the former Water Research Association, being a private company limited by guarantee. The convergence of research interests in waste treatment, water supply, and resource development reflected the organisational change at regional level, but the collection and analysis of hydrologic data were separated off and passed to the Water Data Unit and responsibility for demand forecasting and development planning went to the Central Water Planning Unit.

The national arrangements for data collection, research and planning, as they stand in 1978, are curious and confused. Old unities achieved under the Water Resources Board have been lost, and new ones established, as in the Water Research Centre. No one national organisation stands above the others. Indeed their differing statuses – private company, statutory body, central government unit – make it difficult to see their precise relations.

The *Review* noted a lack of adequate central guidance and monitoring and proposed a much stronger central authority, the National Water Authority, bringing together the National Water Council, the Water Research Centre and the Central Water Planning Unit. The Water Data Unit would continue to provide information for the Department of the Environment, with new provisions made within the National Water Authority to meet data needs there.

These proposals, still under discussion, aim to re-establish a statutory, independent, central organisation embracing most aspects of water research and planning at national level and capable of preparing a national strategy for water services. They would also give the new National Water Authority reserve powers to require the implementation of schemes central to the national strategy, if any Water Authority does not cooperate willingly.

Water and society

The management of water is not an end in itself. It is a means of satisfying certain of society's wants, and of course society wants much else besides more and better water services. Simultaneously with increased water supplies it wants to preserve farm land and an undisturbed landscape in areas of natural beauty. It wants to get rid of the liquid wastes of industrial activity without much expense, and yet enjoy clean rivers and good fishing. Resentment at restrictions on water consumption in times of drought is matched by infuriation when water charges are increased to finance new source development.

The water services may themselves be in conflict, as we have seen in chapter 1, the maximum provision of one precluding the maximum provision of another. On a larger scale the provision of water services may be in conflict with other goals of society – conservation of the environment, overall reduction of public expenditure, increased expenditure in other sectors – alternative goals again not necessarily compatible one with another. One must ask, therefore, how are the different water wants or aims articulated *within* the water management institutions, and how are they articulated *outside*, where water management comes into contact with other regional or national interests?

The membership of the Water Authorities is the key to the first question. Although the size of the governing Boards varies, from fourteen plus chairman in the cases of Wessex and the South West to over fifty for the Thames Water Authority, there are common characteristics of membership. Rather more than half the members are nominated by local authorities and represent the consumers of the services supplied by the Water Authorities. The customers, their wants and their willingness to pay are thus directly represented on the decision-making body. Since these same people are the consumers and financers of other regional services, the articulation of wider, water/non-water issues is also possible within the confines of the Water Authority. The other members of the Boards are appointed by the Minister of Agriculture, Fisheries and Food and the Secretary of State for the Environment (or, in the case of the Welsh National Water Development Authority, the Secretary of State for Wales). The Ministerial appointees are differently qualified for membership. They bring special knowledge of water management problems, sometimes at regional, sometimes at national level, a complement to the local and generally non-technical interests of the local authority nominees.

When a Water Authority has settled on a plan to improve water services, it has to win central government approval for its capital expenditure. Proposals for all but the smallest capital expenditures have to be approved, by the Ministry of Agriculture in the case of land drainage and flood protection works (many of which are grant-aided), and by the Department of the Environment in other cases. The Ministers may order a public inquiry to investigate objections to a proposal, and several of the final authorisations resulting from this procedure have imposed a degree of compromise otherwise unobtainable.

Many proposals for source development involve substantial changes of land use – in a word, flooding. Opposition to reservoir construction has been immense, as we shall see in the next chapter. The Countryside Commission and the Nature Conservancy Council are the national bodies principally concerned to see that land and wildlife interests are not endangered by water development plans. In the past water engineers tended to ignore land/water conflicts until a battle was forced on them. Remembrance of the bitterness of earlier engagements now encourages earlier negotiation between the potential combatants, though combatants they may remain until the dispute is adjudicated.

When proposing capital works for water supply, the Water Authorities can place a private Bill before Parliament and face their opponents in the debating chambers and committee rooms. The fate of any such Bill is unpredictable, since Members' alignments may be unknown at the start and in any case are liable to change as the debates proceed. The alternative procedure, and in general the preferred one now, is to put the matter into the hands of the Secretary of State for the Environment, by requesting a Water Order under the Water Act 1945.

The decision whether or not to act on a Water Authority proposal for capital works is taken externally. Central government, in either its executive or its legislative capacity, determines whether the expenditure is an appropriate use of public funds and whether the proposal will provide the desired water services without undue damage to other interests. The Water Authorities are powerless to spend money on and build capital works without higher authorisation.

The Water Authorities are monopolies, the sole providers of water services, and are able to fix their own charges, but they are closely regulated monopolies, customer-controlled from within through their local authority membership and controlled from without by Ministers answerable to Parliament. And here again is an example of impermanence: the nature of Ministerial control is likely to alter. Strict monitoring of capital expenditure will not be relaxed, but the proposals for the National Water Authority imply a lessening of direct Ministerial control of some other areas of Water

Authority business. The Ministers' overall responsibility will remain, but a strong National Water Authority, empowered to draw up and implement a national policy for water services, could release their Departments from much of their day to day involvement. The complete restructuring of the water industry in 1974 has not made it proof against further change this decade.

CHAPTER 3

SOURCE DEVELOPMENT FOR THE SUPPLY OF MANCHESTER

Of all water services the most fundamental is the provision of water for domestic purposes – drinking, cooking and washing – provision which has probably always required some degree of communal effort. Roman towns in England had organised water supplies and in the medieval period many urban and ecclesiastical authorities took on water supply functions, as is shown by charters dating from the first half of the fifteenth century for the towns of Southampton, Kingston upon Hull and Bath (Central Advisory Water Committee 1963:1). The growing demand for water during the Industrial Revolution led to a proliferation of water supply agencies, faced with the task of providing ever greater volumes of water at a time when local supplies were diminishing rapidly through over-abstraction and pollution. The problem in Manchester was as acute as anywhere, and the water agency turned for supplies first to the Pennine hills and then to the Lake District.

In 1848 Manchester was the first of the industrial towns to undertake a large upland impounding scheme, and Liverpool and Birmingham soon followed its example. By the end of the nineteenth century a new pattern of water supply was widely established, with towns drawing their supplies from distant, uncontaminated gathering grounds in the hills. Manchester's imagination and enterprise were well rewarded: its water supply schemes were so successful that the supply area, centred on the newly incorporated city, was enlarged again and again to take in peripheral townships. Other water agencies were taken over by Manchester Corporation Waterworks and by 1974, when in turn that organisation disappeared into the North West Water Authority, it served a population of around 1.25 million, as well as supplying water in bulk to many communities lying close to the aqueducts from the Lake District. In all as many as 1.75 million received water wholly or partly through the efforts of Manchester Corporation Waterworks.

Manchester's supply system was typical of many set up around the turn of the century. It was both capital intensive and inflexible. The structures were huge pieces of engineering, designed to operate in a particular way which it is now difficult to alter. The natural system which distributes water by means of the rivers was by-passed completely. It was also characteristic in that it was planned, financed and executed by a local organisation to meet local needs. Only since the implementation of the Water Act 1973 has the system been incorporated into a larger, regional programme for water supply in the North West.

Manchester was attracted to the Lake District in the 1870s because its clean, soft water could be used without treatment. Land use and public access within the gathering grounds were strictly controlled to prevent contamination. A major change in management, unrelated to the replacement of the Waterworks by the Water Authority, is the opening up of the gathering grounds and the reservoirs as treatment facilities are interposed between source and consumer.

Another change is the preference for the regulated but otherwise natural lake as a water source in place of the impounding dam and reservoir. To a certain degree, physical circumstances caused the Ullswater and Windermere developments of the 1960s to differ from the earlier Thirlmere and Haweswater impoundments, but the difference also results from the Lake District's intense opposition to reservoir construction and from the Waterworks' desire to secure water without, if possible, further destruction of the landscape. However, large natural lakes suitable for controlled abstraction are not always to be found, and tentative proposals for future water developments in the North West region include a reversion to the dam and reservoir principle for the enlargement of Haweswater.

Until now the system has been used entirely for direct supply via aqueduct. This is the only way of getting Lakeland water to Manchester, since the river network gives no natural route. As the Lakeland sources are relieved of their obligation to serve Manchester and can be deployed in conjunction with other sources to serve the whole region, a less rigid, less artificial pattern of use is possible. A change already proposed is that more water be put into the rivers, to increase and regulate their flow so there can be abstraction, return and reuse along their length, to the advantage of in-channel uses too.

Another consequence of the 1973 legislation is the integration of water supply with all other water services. While water supply was the only function of a water undertaker it was inevitable that source development was carried out in disregard of issues of river basin management, pollution control and water reuse. The Water Authorities' conjunction of functions permits water supply to be put back into its natural context.

Our area of study enlarges progressively: from the township of Manchester, through the area supplied with water by Manchester Corporation Waterworks, to the region served by the North West Water Authority. A final question is whether this last unit of management, the North West region, is the most appropriate. It has come about through the coalescence of River Authorities, water undertakers and sewage authorities. In all 231 separate units have been replaced by this single Water Authority, a reorganisation convulsive enough for the staff concerned without any further suggestion that the unit might be too small. But in water supply the North West is not self-sufficient. Since the 1880s Liverpool has been importing water from

North Wales (upper Severn) and today this makes a very substantial contribution to the North West's total resource, even more than the Lake District. One Authority does not have control over all the North West's water sources despite the reorganisation, and briefly in this chapter and again in chapter 8 we consider inter-regional and national aspects of water supply.

The early development of Manchester's water supply

The history of Manchester's water supply can be traced back to the beginning of the sixteenth century, when a spring in Fountain Street was linked by aqueduct to an open conduit in the centre of the township, over a distance of half a mile or so. Pressure of demand led the Court Leet in 1578 to fix the daily ration per household to that which a woman could carry in a vessel on her head. By 1775 the spring had dried up and other local water sources were unable to meet the growing need. The Manchester and Salford Waterworks Company, founded in 1809 as a private company, built Manchester's first reservoirs at Gorton, but the increased supply was soon outstripped by demand and in 1847 surveying officers recorded: 'All the medical witnesses agree that the large rate of mortality by which Manchester is distinguished is greatly owing to the destitution of water'. (quoted in Manchester Corporation Waterworks 1974a: 1). The Waterworks Company was taken into public ownership the same year, and the Parliamentary Act authorising this also authorised reservoir construction in the Longdendale valley, in the Pennine foothills about fifteen miles east of Manchester. Site work started the following year and in 1851 the first upland water was brought into the city centre (Manchester Corporation Waterworks 1974b). A complex of seven reservoirs, flood water channels and aqueducts was constructed in Longdendale over a period of thirty-three years, for its time an exceptionally sophisticated system and one which established Manchester as a pioneer in municipal water supply (figure 8).

During the 1870s it was apparent that population and water consumption per head were both rising so rapidly that Longdendale alone, successful though this development was, could not meet demand into the 1880s. Another large catchment and store of water was needed. None was to be found nearby and Manchester had to look farther afield. It was natural that attention should focus on the Lake District which receives England's highest rainfall and could, like Longdendale, deliver water by gravity, and Manchester was not alone in considering the Lakes as potential sources of supply.

Messrs Hemans and Hassard, in evidence to the Royal Commission on Water Supply (1869), proposed the damming of Thirlmere and Haweswater, the conversion of Ullswater into a balancing, distributing reservoir, and the conveyance of Lakeland water over 270 miles to London, but these metropolitan suggestions were not pursued.

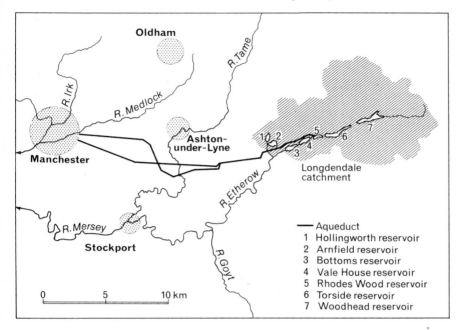

Figure 8   Manchester's reservoirs in Longdendale.

J. F. la Trobe Bateman, who had planned and directed the Longdendale project, at first proposed joint supply of Manchester and Liverpool from Ullswater and Haweswater, but Liverpool Corporation chose instead to investigate development of its own source in the Vyrnwy valley in North Wales, and Manchester proceeded alone in the Lake District. In 1876 Bateman was asked to report on the possibility of supplying Manchester from Thirlmere, a hundred miles away.

Bateman reported favourably and immediately the Manchester Waterworks Committee resolved to promote Bateman's scheme. The Committee also decided that: 'if the difficulty, annoyance and expense which they had experienced in connection with the Longdendale works were to be avoided in connection with this scheme, and the entire control of the water secured, it was necessary that the whole drainage area, from the crown of the mountains down into the valley, should be purchased' (Harwood 1895: 36). The purchase of an entire catchment was then unprecedented. (To protect the supply which passes untreated to Manchester the public is still denied access to the lake, and land use in the lower part of the catchment is strictly regulated.)

The potential benefits to Manchester did not impress Thirlmere landowners and the purchase of land and water rights was rigorously opposed locally. There were two ancient Manors in the catchment, Wythburn and

Legburgthwaite. Mr Thomas Leathes, Lord of the Manor of Legburgth-waite, owner of Dale Head Estate and of the lake, was especially antagonistic to the scheme which was carried forward only after his death. Sir John James Harwood described how he and Alderman Graves, members of the Manchester Waterworks Committee, anxious to see the margin of the lake but refused entry to Leathes' land: 'one very wet day . . . went over from Keswick, and to avoid observation . . . crept on our hands and knees past Dale Head Hall down to the Lake. We had to return to Keswick in our wet clothes and the consequence was that I was laid up for a week afterwards from a cold' (Harwood 1895: 55).

The Thirlmere Defence Association likewise fought the proposals. Objecting to the introduction of large scale engineering works into the Lake District, the Association pointed out in its appeal for support that a Parliamentary inquiry would normally confine itself to the arguments of the promoters on the one side and the opposing landowners on the other, ignoring aesthetic considerations altogether. Partly as a result of these agitations, preservationist arguments were put forward both in the Parliamentary debates and to the specially constituted Select Committee which considered the Manchester Corporation Bill for the Thirlmere scheme.

In all thirty-three petitions against the Bill were heard, and though the outcome was essentially favourable to Manchester the Act of 1879 was different in one important respect from the Bill as originally presented. The Select Committee was satisfied that the water of Thirlmere could be used without detriment to the public enjoyment of the Lake District and suggested no alterations to the proposals for the dam and reservoir. (Not everyone agreed with this finding, of course, and the reaction to the construction contributed to the founding of the National Trust for Places of Historic Interest or Natural Beauty, in 1895.) Rather it was to the aqueduct proposals that the Select Committee proposed changes.

Various towns and rural districts between the Lake District and Manchester, near the line of the aqueduct, had asked to be supplied from Thirlmere if the Manchester scheme was carried through, taking up a general recommendation of the Royal Commission on Water Supply (1869) that when a town supplies itself from a distant source by pipeline or conduit provision ought to be made for the supply of all places along the route. The Prince of Wales, as President of the Society of Arts, had also commented on the need to use major sources of water not merely for the benefit of a few large centres of population but for the advantage of the whole nation. Manchester Corporation found it prudent not to object to the suggestions that it supply water in bulk to intermediate communities and to interpret this wider demand for Thirlmere water as a 'striking testimony in favour of the public utility of the scheme' (Harwood 1895: 114). When the Act was passed in 1879 Manchester became the country's first bulk supply authority. Thus, instead of being a water-tight link to Manchester, the aqueduct was perforated at intervals and water drawn off for nearby communities who made annual payments to Manchester for this service.

Even before the Act was passed a trade depression in Manchester and the surrounding region – and some wet weather – was beginning to reduce the urgency of the Thirlmere scheme. Water consumption did not increase in the manner predicted, and in consequence neither did the revenue from the water rates. Construction was delayed, and the foundation stone of the Thirlmere dam was not laid until 1890. Three years later the first Lakeland water arrived in Manchester, to be received with ceremony at a temporary fountain outside the Town Hall.

This short history of the Thirlmere scheme shows many of the general characteristics of England's municipal water supply until the middle of this century: the source in a wet upland area where a simple impounding structure stored a large volume of water; restricted public access in the catchment to save the supply from contamination; early and organised opposition to engineering interference in an area of natural beauty; the arrangement of supplies in bulk for the region as well as in detail for the large town; and above all the initiative of the water undertaker, obliged by statute to provide water but without any government assistance to find it at a distance when local supplies run out.

The Ullswater controversy

It was originally hoped that Thirlmere and Longdendale together would meet Manchester's water needs well into this century, but the unsought-for bulk supply commitments reduced the resources available for Manchester and by 1916 it was looking for an additional water source in the Lakes. Haweswater was chosen and again the entire catchment was purchased and protected, this time without difficulty since the lake and catchment belonged to a single owner willing to sell. The enabling Act was passed in 1919 but because of a depressed economy construction was delayed, started, halted and restarted, and supplies from Haweswater did not reach Manchester until 1941. Then the water came via the Thirlmere aqueduct but in 1955 a second aqueduct direct from Haweswater allowed more water to be taken (figure 9). During the severe drought of 1959 Manchester and its aqueduct-linked communities were well supplied, while other towns in the region were rationed to emergency levels.

The Haweswater scheme, with its supplementary reservoir in Wet Sleddale, planned and authorised in the 1910s, was seen to be insufficient for long-term needs even before the Haweswater aqueduct was finished, and in 1960 Ullswater was considered as a third Lakeland source. The controversy which flared around the Ullswater proposals entirely changed the nature of surface water development in the Lake District. The preservationist cause, still remembering its defeat at Thirlmere, was so strengthened that the eventual

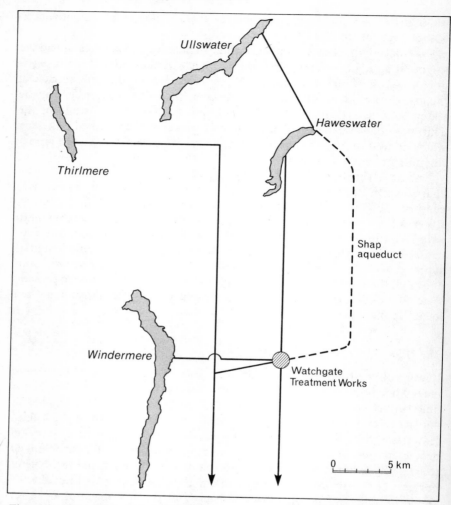

Figure 9   Manchester's Lake District sources and aqueducts.

development of Ullswater was permitted only with the most stringent conditions to minimise disturbance.

Manchester's difficulties began when its water engineers surveyed Ullswater surreptitiously and were spotted by local residents. There already existed a society to protect Ullswater from water skiers and this, the Ullswater Preservation Society, soon rose to the greater challenge of the water supply scheme. Not that Manchester's proposals were well understood in the Lake District. The Waterworks did not attempt to identify the interested groups and explain its proposals to them. Instead an impersonal and ambiguous press notice was issued in September 1961: 'Among the proposals now being investigated are dams and reservoirs in the Bannisdale and Borrow Beck areas, north and east of Kendal; a possible intake scheme from Ullswater and possible catchments north and west of the existing Lake District sources' (quoted in Dolbey 1974: 77). The technical pros and cons of the proposals were not at issue locally because they were not known. Opposition rested on the argument that *any* engineering interference would destroy amenity and reduce access, both unacceptable in an area designated a National Park. Local authorities, the Cumberland and Lancashire River Boards and many local and national amenity groups joined forces with the Ullswater Preservation Society, but Manchester Corporation appears to have dismissed the opposition as inevitable, and inevitably ineffective.

A scheme for a movable weir at Ullswater's outfall to the River Eamont and for abstraction from the controlled lake was put forward as Part III of a Manchester Corporation Bill in 1961. Manchester saw a difference between what it proposed for Ullswater and the traditional dam and reservoir development already carried out at Thirlmere and Haweswater and proposed in the same Bill for Bannisdale. The opposition saw no such difference. Ullswater was to be developed for water supply: Manchester was once again invading the Lake District. Lord Birkett who opened the debate in the House of Lords advocated opposition *in principle*, and he was successful in that the Bill was denied a second reading and never reached a Committee for detailed examination of the evidence for and against.

The Ullswater scheme was defeated, but of course the need for water remained. In 1964 Manchester made a second attempt, using a different legal strategy and different tactics in the field. This time no Bill was placed before Parliament. Instead the Corporation applied to the Minister of Housing and Local Government for a Water Order, under the Water Act 1945 and the Town and Country Planning Act 1962. There was a public inquiry in Kendal in the summer of 1965 and the Minister's verdict was given the following year. The other significant change was Manchester's concern about its public image in the Lake District. The Corporation engaged a firm of public relations consultants to help here. There were occasional press conferences and bulletins in the local press explaining the need for the scheme and emphasising that there was to be no reservoir, no change in appearance of the lake and its shore and no restrictions on access. Manchester forced the Lake District away from its ignorance of technical and amenity aspects of the proposals but great local animosity remained. An example of this was the refusal of Kendal hoteliers to provide food or accommodation for the proponents of the scheme during the public inquiry. The scheme's supporters stayed in Windermere and their food was bought and prepared privately.

The proposals investigated at the inquiry were for developments at Ullswater and Windermere, to draw off water when lake levels and outflows were above prescribed minima and to deliver it to a treatment works to be built at Watchgate, near Kendal. Ullswater supplies would pass first into Haweswater and then through a new aqueduct from Haweswater to Watchgate along Longsleddale, needed to increase capacity above that of the Longsleddale section of the original Haweswater aqueduct. The earlier proposal for a reservoir in Bannisdale had been abandoned, largely on amenity grounds, the movable weir for Ullswater's outfall was also omitted, and the pumping stations at Windermere and Ullswater were now planned as underground features with silent running equipment, invisible and inaudible from the outside.

There were four essential elements in the proposals: Ullswater abstraction; Windermere abstraction; treatment works and control centre at Watchgate; and a second pipeline down the Longsleddale valley. Manchester Corporation already owned the Watchgate site and had outline planning permission for its development, so three elements remained to be decided. When the Minister gave his decision in May 1966 it was 2:1 in favour of Manchester. Ullswater and Windermere abstractions were permitted and the Longsleddale pipeline was rejected.

Without a new aqueduct the additional water could not be conveyed for treatment and distribution, so the bottleneck in the system had to be removed. An alternative aqueduct route was sought and found along the line of the A6 Shap road. A Water Order for the Shap Aqueduct was granted in 1974 and it is being built now, on a route which skirts the boundary of the Lake District National Park. Another difference from the original route is that whereas water moves through Longsleddale under gravity, it has to be pumped over Shap, with increased operating costs.

The development eventually allowed at Ullswater was very closely controlled to preserve the unspoilt condition of the lake and the surrounding country. To make sure that disturbance was minimal the initial design was modified and the Minister retained control over each stage of the work by authorising expenditure not *en bloc* but as each preceding stage was completed to his satisfaction.

The previous mistrust of Manchester was reflected in the Minister's decision about the conditions under which abstraction could take place. Manchester had proposed to pump when levels were above the prescribed minima, levels to be measured at a new gauging station. The Minister insisted on an additional, physical control to make over-pumping impossible. An underground labyrinth weir has been built at the intake, and all who are interested can see that when the lake falls to the critical level no water flows into the pumping station. Neat though the device is, it is unnecessary except for psychological reassurance.

The difficult circumstances in which Manchester's water engineers were working show themselves again in the siting of the Ullswater pumping station. Preliminary field surveys were very limited, and only when the Water Order was granted and work began on site could deep borings be taken of local geology. Then thick layers of unconsolidated glacial material were found, containing water to within a metre or two of the surface and giving exceptionally troublesome conditions in which to excavate a chamber 20 metres below ground level. To prevent flooding and collapse of the side walls as excavation proceeded, a new construction technique 'diaphragm walling' was used for the first time in this country. A pre-construction survey would almost certainly have led to a search for an alternative site.

Figure 10 shows the underground pumping station, encircled by the diaphragm wall of steel-reinforced concrete. It was landscaped into the existing contours and now, with a full grass cover, it is invisible from the ground, from the lake or from the air. Nor does the access road reveal its presence. The original narrow stone-walled lane was preserved over most of its length, with minor straightenings and the addition of passing places to enable contractors' lorries to creep through. Disturbance of the landscape has been such that only those visitors conducted to the site are likely to find it.

It is difficult to determine the costs of amenity preservation in the Ullswater scheme, though clearly they are large. The cheaper alternatives of a surface pumping station, as proposed in 1961, and purpose built roads were impossible after the defeat of the Manchester Bill. Only an underground pumping station sufficed, but how much of the £1.4 million spent on it is attributable to amenity preservation is hard to say. An equivalent structure on the surface was not costed. £250,000 is a figure given for amenity and landscaping aspects of the entire Ullswater scheme, but this is just for 'trimmings', contouring, vegetation replacement and so on, and takes no account of the fact that amenity considerations determined some of the scheme's most fundamental features.

There was no question of restricting public access to either Ullswater or Windermere, in the catchment or on the water surface, since both lakes were already important tourist attractions. The cleanliness of water at source, central features of the Thirlmere and Haweswater developments, could not be maintained for Ullswater and Windermere. The Watchgate treatment works having been built from necessity, there is now the possibility of releasing the original protected catchments from some of their pollution controls. Unprotected water from Ullswater passes into Haweswater and all water taken from Haweswater is treated at Watchgate. There have been several proposals for greater public use of Haweswater, and one likely to be implemented soon is for a picnic area and new road on the north shore. Several of the Longdendale reservoirs in the Pennines, formerly protected, have already been opened to public use on completion of treatment works. Thirlmere water is to be treated too, and when this is effected, by about 1980, the movement away from protected sources towards public use and subsequent water treatment will be complete.

What type of public use is appropriate in the newly released catchments and lakes is a matter for determination with planning and recreation auth-

Plan

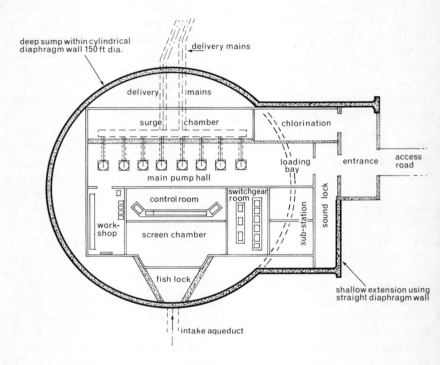

Section

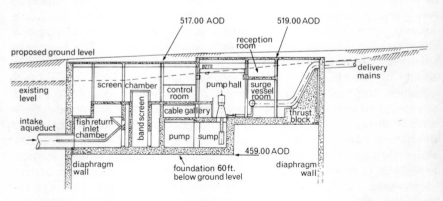

Figure 10   The Ullswater pumping station.
Source: Manchester Corporation Waterworks 1969:8.

orities. On grounds quite other than pollution prevention some restrictions on access might be justified, for instance to preserve peaceful, little visited areas away from the mainstream of holiday motor traffic, but most restrictions like this would be indirect, effected through the non-provision of tourist facilities.

The Lake District and Manchester are at present on good terms, thanks to the sensitive landscaping of the Ullswater, Windermere and Watchgate developments and the promised opening up first of Haweswater and then of Thirlmere. But in the suggestions for public use of Haweswater can be seen the underlying and continuing conflict. Investment in permanent buildings such as restaurants or toilet blocks would seem in order, except that it is proposed that the Haweswater source be increased in the future by raising the lake level more than 35 metres (Water Resources Board 1973a vol 1: 58). Permanent lakeside buildings, including the existing Haweswater Hotel, would be drowned and, although the enlargement proposal is so far most tentative, plans for the north shore picnic site include portable buildings only.

Conflicts of interest in the development of inland surface storage

Resentment at Manchester's activities in the Lake District is part of a nationwide conflict over the creation of inland surface water storage. The Lakes used for water supply show two different aspects of storage. One is reservoir construction, involving the enlargement of natural lakes with concomitant drowning of land and settlements and a water surface fluctuating very considerably with the pumping regime. The other is the pumping of natural lakes to lower the surface a little but frequently below former levels. Each has aroused intense opposition in the Lake District, although the former causes more disturbance than the latter, in both construction and operation.

The controversies over the Ullswater scheme in the period 1961 to 1962 showed that objections were not necessarily directly related to the disturbance the developments would cause and that the most vociferous opponents were not necessarily those most at risk. In the case of the first Ullswater scheme one of the reasons for these disparities was the objectors' ignorance of the nature of the scheme, an ignorance partly real, partly feigned. When development plans are widely publicised, with the objectives and methods of management explained, opposition tends to be less hysterical, settling upon substantial issues of conflicting land demands which do not disappear even with good public relations.

Today new surface storage does not require the purchase of the catchment area by the water developers and so the problems formerly encountered in this transaction no longer arise. However, others have replaced them, so much so that development is more difficult than previously, with the Ullswater proposals in 1962 and the Farndale scheme in the North York

Moors National Park in 1970 being dramatically rejected. The Water Resources Board (1973a vol 1: 2) admitted that the National Parks raised special difficulties but found it impossible to avoid the Parks completely for inland surface storage. Only the maximum use of estuary storage gives a long-term alternative, and estuary storage of course brings its own problems.

With the more common type of inland storage, the reservoir, the conflicts are first with the people who will be displaced, whose land or home will be flooded. The loss of a farming valley beneath the surface of a reservoir sounds a more tragic note than does the demolition of urban property in the path of a motorway, but the principle is the same. The wellbeing of the larger community is put before that of the smaller displaced group. Our society has accepted much of this compulsory relocation as unavoidable, and the main debates have centred on the magnitude of compensation and the type of assistance to be given to help people establish a new life elsewhere. Yet land flooded for a reservoir ceases to be land, and this, together with the large areas involved, has exacerbated the feeling that the taking of land for reservoirs is a special case and is seriously reducing the nation's stock of farmland and wilderness.

The loss of good quality farmland is taken so seriously now that a moratorium has been suggested on reservoir construction in lowland England, where topography produces comparatively extensive, shallow reservoirs. 'No new surface storage in the south east' was a feature of one development programme considered by the Water Resources Board (1973a vol 2: 55). In upland areas the loss to farming may be less on account of the lower productivity of the land and the deeper, narrower reservoirs created, but the loss to amenity may be very much greater.

On open moorland a reservoir may drown the only trees, as the Errwood reservoir has done in the Goyt valley of the Peak District (Peak Park Planning Board 1971: 2). Such a loss is not made good by afforestation of the valley slopes, something frequently undertaken by the Forestry Commission and others. The moor ecology as well as the riverine trees is destroyed, and even in existing wooded valleys afforestation generally involves the substitution of conifers for hardwoods.

Another ecological tragedy is the drowning of unique plant assemblages, such as those lost beneath the reservoir at Cow Green in the upper Tees valley. The Cow Green site lay partly in the Upper Teesdale National Nature Reserve, partly in an area designated as of 'special scientific interest'. Arguments for its preservation were advanced by the Natural Environment Research Council and the National Parks Commission, but a long and informed dialogue between the parties in the mid-1960s could not resolve the fundamental problem that an irreplaceable scientific asset was also the only site that could be developed in time to meet Teesside's water needs in the 1970s (Arvill 1967: 125–7, 305). The reservoir was authorised in 1967 and is now in service, regulating flow in the upper Tees.

All reservoir development entails loss of land, with the degree of conflict depending largely on the value placed on its existing use. Natural lakes developed for water supply escape this problem, but share with reservoirs that of 'drawdown' or lowering of the water surface to expose the foreshore. Pumping from Ullswater and Windermere is carefully controlled to minimise disturbance. Water levels and effects at the lake margins were much discussed before the Windermere/Ullswater Order was granted, but it was experience with the Lake District reservoirs that had made people so sensitive in planning the operation of the new regulated lakes. Water levels in Thirlmere and Haweswater fluctuate a great deal, in dry periods exposing tens of metres of foreshore. In the drought of 1973 the reservoirs were only one third full and at Haweswater the remains of Mardale village were uncovered for the first time since their submergence in 1940.

Reservoir and lake drawdown are probably most unsightly if the margins are shallow and in soft material, and here too the shore-line ecology is most likely to suffer, but aside from any aesthetic or ecological considerations drawdown can be a nuisance to water-based recreation. Boating, fishing, swimming and water-side picnicing are often offered as benefits of reservoir construction and, while this may be 'coals to Newcastle' in the Lake District, a reservoir may indeed be a gain in amenity in an area with few expanses of inland water. If at the period of peak recreation demand the water level plummets, leaving a long, muddy beach in front of shore-line buildings and only shallow water over irregularities in the valley floor, both enjoyment and safety are jeopardised. Thus, when a new reservoir is built and offered for public recreation, its operating procedures must take some account of the water levels required for recreation. If construction has been justified on the grounds that the reservoir will serve dual functions, maximum operating efficiency in the water supply aspect may have to be sacrificed.

The unpredictability of the eventual development decision, if opposing interests are irreconcilable, is encouraging earlier and more detailed consultation between land and water interests in the hopes that an agreed set of least objectionable sites may be found before a final development proposal is advanced. Throughout its life the Water Resources Board consulted countryside and amenity interests about proposals it was formulating, and the National Water Council and the Water Authorities are maintaining and strengthening this liaison. Yet liaison cannot remove conflict when this is firmly based: much opposition to inland surface water storage is real and justified. The solutions proposed by the Water Resources Board were to reduce the need for new surface storage as much as possible by enlarging or redeploying existing reservoirs and by developing underground storage and then, when new reservoirs must be built, to restrict construction to a small number of large sites (Water Resources Board 1973a vol 1: 2).

The Water Space Amenity Commission, set up in 1974, is also founded on the belief that by coming together in discussion the interested parties will increase their awareness of each others' problems, and so promote amicable, multiple use of water storage. The representation of both active and passive recreational interests alongside those of water supply must surely lead to a more informed debate, even if it cannot produce simple answers.

Public supply in the reorganised water industry

Before the implementation of the Water Act in April 1974 Manchester Corporation owned the sources in the Lake District, together with the aqueducts linking them to consumers. Costs of purchasing land, constructing works and maintaining and operating them were met mainly from Manchester's rates. Contributions of capital and annual income came from the communities with bulk supply agreements with Manchester, but in comparison with Manchester their part ownership of resources and entitlement to supplies was small. Manchester Corporation Waterworks was one of 180 water undertakers in England and Wales prior to 1974, separate from the River Authorities but with overlapping responsibilities for providing water.

Under the Water Resources Act 1963 the River Authorities had the duty to conserve, redistribute or otherwise augment water resources in their area, but unlike the water undertakers they had no statutory obligation on them to find more water. The water undertakers had the statutory obligation but no control over their new sources. A water undertaker could not abstract water from a source except under licence from the River Authority, and it happened sometimes that a River Authority chose on general grounds of water conservation to license a source other than that preferred by the water undertaker, or to delay issuing a licence until it had itself investigated alternative sources or carried out development schemes. The Wilson Committee argued: 'If a body is under a statutory obligation to supply water, then either it must itself have the powers to enable it to meet this obligation, or there must be another body which has a statutory obligation to make water available to it.' (Central Advisory Water Committee 1971: 38).

While the water undertakers were at a disadvantage over new sources, the River Authorities were at a disadvantage over existing works for direct supply. Water undertakers were entitled to licences of right, which could be varied by the River Authorities only if compensation was paid or alternative sources found. In almost all cases the effect of the 1963 Act was to sanctify the undertakers' source use and patterns of supply. Amalgamations of undertakers continued, their number reducing from over 1000 in 1956 to around 180 in 1974, with some redeployment of resources as a result, but the undertakers remained the masters of their own sources. They also enjoyed complete control of the distribution networks, for the River Authorities had no powers of acquisition or alteration of their method of operation.

Greater flexibility was needed to effect three changes: the conversion of direct supply reservoirs to river regulators; the use of one source in conjunction with others, changing from one to another during the year to maintain yields; and the redeployment of the distribution network so that a source could be switched from supplying one area to supplying another. It was not that a nationwide juggling of sources and supply areas was required, for many supply patterns were perfectly appropriate, but in the cases where change was desirable it was hindered. The Water Act 1973 was framed to rectify this.

When the Act was implemented, Manchester Corporation Waterworks was absorbed into the North West Water Authority, disappearing like all those water undertakers run by local authorities either singly or through joint boards. A minority of water undertakers were statutory water companies and these survived, acting as agents of the Water Authorities. There were none in existence in the North West, however, where the Water Authority has full control of all internal water sources and aqueducts. The survival elsewhere of twenty-nine water companies (and one in Jersey) is not easy to explain, except in terms of a Conservative government's relucance to take over £250 million of private capital (Secretary of State for the Environment 1971). The *Review of the Water Industry in England and Wales* contained proposals to integrate the private companies with the Water Authorities to end this anomaly (Department of the Environment *etc.* 1976).

Tentative proposals for future uses of the Lake District sources include regulation of the River Lune, either from an enlarged Haweswater or from a new reservoir in Borrowdale (figure 11). The Lune is presently an important water source, managed together with underground sources in the Lancashire Conjunctive Use Scheme, and the regulation of its flow by releases from upstream surface storage would permit further river abstractions and increase the yield of the Conjunctive Use Scheme. Comparing the Haweswater and Borrowdale alternatives, the Water Resources Board favoured an enlargement of Haweswater. Borrowdale, although just outside the Park, is in an unspoilt valley of high amenity value. The Board preferred to leave Borrowdale untouched and to confine development to the already disturbed Haweswater.

The 1974 reorganisation has also made possible the partial redeployment of Thirlmere. At present all the Thirlmere supply goes south into the aqueduct. A change in use is already authorised, whereby part of this water is put into the Cumberland Derwent, draining north and west to Workington, when population and industrial growth in West Cumbria eventually demands an additional water supply there.

Manchester Corporation Waterworks had the longest history of any water undertaker committed to bulk supplies, but in 1974 all bulk supply agreements were terminated. Obviously termination of an agreement does not mean termination of supply, but it does mean that for the first time the use

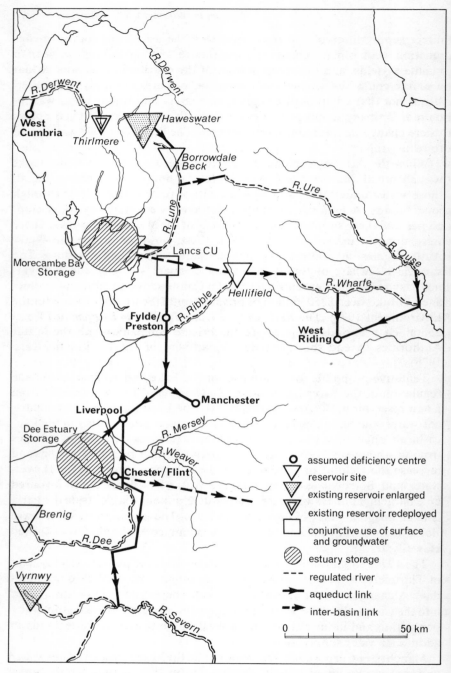

Figure 11 Some proposals for an integrated supply system for the North West.
Based on Water Resources Board 1973a vol 1: map 5.

of the distribution network can be varied, an essential change if sources and demands, existing and new, are to be matched properly. Ossified supply patterns, some of them dating from the 1879 Thirlmere Act, can be replaced by patterns presently appropriate and capable of change with future circumstances. The Thirlmere and Haweswater aqueducts, the latter extended by the new Shap aqueduct, will remain central features of the network, but the Lancashire Conjunctive Use Scheme is increasing supplies in the middle of the region so that Lakeland water can be partly redeployed north and westwards in Cumbria and perhaps even eastwards over the Pennines into the tributaries of the Yorkshire Ouse.

Just what redeployment and new development is needed depends upon growth of demand, within the region as a whole and at particular localities, and part of the North West Water Authority's resource planning unit is engaged in demand forecasting. Here and elsewhere in England and Wales statistical records of public water supplies are quite brief, with certain fragmentary data from 1955 and more comprehensive information from 1960. There was almost no quantitative information on direct industrial and agricultural abstractions of water until after the Water Resources Act 1963. Such a data base does not justify the use of very sophisticated extrapolation techniques: regression analysis and subjective judgement together produce the trend lines from which forecasts are made.

The predictions on which the original Thirlmere and Haweswater schemes were based were not fulfilled as quickly as expected. More recent forecasts, including those of the Water Resources Board (1973a vol 1:25–35), are similar and have been revised downwards to take account of a falling off in demand for metered supplies to industry since 1971 and of population stabilisation. Price too could affect demand, and some argue that indeed price should be used deliberately as a demand regulator (Russell 1974 and discussion following).

Nationally the demand for public water supplies is growing but on present showing is more likely to have increased by 50 percent at the end of the century than to have doubled, as predicted by the Water Resources Board. It is open to each Water Authority to meet demand through resource development, redeployment or redistribution within its own territory. It is also open to a Water Authority to choose not to meet peak demand in peak years, that is to draw more heavily on existing resources and to reduce their reliability, rationing supplies in critical periods which would in future occur more often.

Another possibility is the importing of water from another Water Authority region. The North West Water Authority is an established net importer, taking supplies for Liverpool and parts of the Wirral and mid-Cheshire from Lake Vyrnwy (Severn–Trent Water Authority) and from the regulated River Dee (Welsh National Water Development Authority). If estuary storage is developed on the lower Dee, as seems possible around the turn of the century, the Welsh and North West Authorities could increase their trade much further.

The reorganised water industry is fully capable of dealing with resource development and allocation problems within the ten Water Authority regions, and this is an immense improvement on the former system of separate River Authorities and water undertakers, but the Water Authorities' individual autonomy does not make the planning of water transfers between regions any easier. One argument advanced for amalgamating existing water agencies into much larger, regional Water Authorities was that the new units would be more nearly self-sufficient in resources. While on a smaller scale this is true, several inter-basin transfers previously between River Authorities being within one Water Authority region, on a larger scale it is not true. Wales has more water than it needs itself and has exported it for nearly a century. In general western England has more water than eastern England, and west–east transfers have much to commend them. Complete regional self-sufficiency would seem to be more costly than a more fluid policy of inter-regional trading.

The present system does not prevent inter-regional trading, but nor does it actively assist it. In chapter 8 the significance of this is discussed more fully in the context of very large source works and river transfer schemes. The point to be made here in connection with public water supplies in the North West is that the new system has not removed all sources of potential conflict between the various water agencies. The North West region is not self-sufficient in water, yet the system ignores this and provides no clear national policy to help it find water beyond its boundaries. Here surely is a parallel with Manchester's predicament a century ago when its local supplies ran out and, on its own initiative, it looked a hundred miles north to the Lake District.

CHAPTER 4

THE ALLOCATION OF WATER FOR SPRAY IRRIGATION

As chapter 1 has pointed out, the second essential function of water management is the allocation of scarce resources among competing users. The previous chapter looked at the first function, the creation of *new* resources by the construction of surface storage and distribution networks. Here we consider the efficient use of *existing* resources. For while it is likely that new sources of supply will continue to be developed to add to the resource base, efficient management of the system as a whole requires that good use be made of what is already there before investing in expensive and often disruptive engineering works to produce more. With or without the development of new resources, competing demands for water must be reconciled and what is currently available in the rivers and aquifers divided fairly between them.*

We can see this allocation problem and the procedures that have come to deal with it by looking at the River Great Ouse basin in East Anglia, where the growth of a comparatively new water demand has put a special strain on supplies in one of the driest regions in the country. This demand is for spray irrigation, an agricultural technique which has developed since the Second World War until it is common practice in south east England and a major consumer of water in the summer months. Figure 12 shows the concentration of the irrigated area here. Perhaps even today the term 'irrigation' is one which most of us associate most readily with semi-desert areas, but in East Anglia puffs and feathers of spray are now a distinctive feature of the summer landscape.

Withers (1973: 137) indicated that irrigation through channels or ditches was perhaps first introduced into England at Babraham in Cambridgeshire, early in the 1560s, and this type of irrigation was quite widely practised in the first half of the nineteenth century. Thereafter the agricultural depression may have been responsible for the apparent decline, for in agricultural journals and reports irrigation is mentioned but rarely. Certainly by the 1930s irrigation had been virtually abandoned, except for the occasional water meadow or fenland field flooded from a higher level stream.

*Here we are discussing the allocation of water at source, the abstraction of water from rivers and aquifers, not the division of the public mains supply between individual households and trade premises.

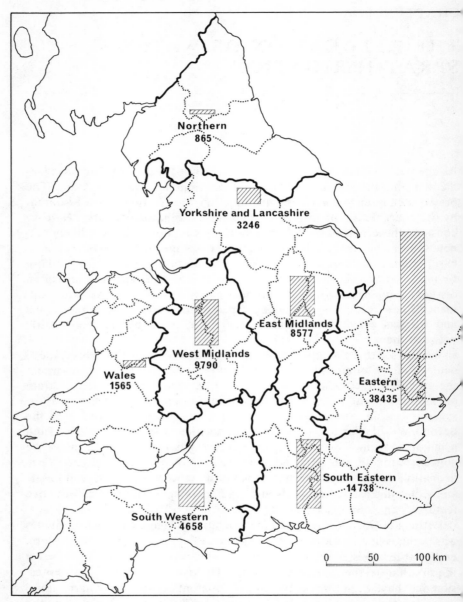

Figure 12   Areas irrigated, by agricultural regions, 1974 (regional totals in hectares). Source: Information from the Ministry of Agriculture, Fisheries and Food, collected from a special inquiry into the practice of irrigation in England and Wales in 1975.

After the Second World War irrigation revived, but with different techniques. Instead of applying water to the soil by simple flooding or by networks of channels, the new irrigation used overhead spraying equipment, delivering water in droplets like rain. Penman's evaporation formula was an important practical aid to the calculation of soil moisture deficits (Penman 1948; Ministry of Agriculture, Fisheries and Food 1954), and through this combination of delicate, controllable equipment and knowledge of soil water requirements, farmers were able for the first time to apply water in quantities calculated to give maximum benefit in terms of crop response. During the 1950s the use of spray irrigation grew steadily, and a long summer drought in 1959 gave it an added impetus. The drought focussed attention on the precariousness of the water supply and on the emergence of this potentially excessive abstraction for spray irrigation. The Sub-Committee on the Growing Demand for Water (Central Advisory Water Committee 1960) suggested that the accelerating demand for spray irrigation would soon put water resources under very severe strain.

Water used for irrigation is incorporated into plant tissue or transpired into the atmosphere and so is lost to the river system. Irrigation is a consumptive use, in contrast to most other uses which recycle water, consuming some but returning a good deal to the river. The uncontrolled abstraction and loss of large quantities of water in a new use, in summer when river and groundwater levels are generally low, may jeopardise the supplies of existing users. By the early 1960s spray irrigation was beginning to upset the balance of water supply and demand in the south east. The remedy adopted and effected through the Water Resources Act 1963 is one of several possible approaches to the water allocation problem. This chapter examines how successful it has been, and looks briefly at some alternatives. While many provisions of the 1963 Act have been repealed in the Water Act 1973, those concerned with water allocation remain largely unchanged: present allocation policy still has its roots in the 1963 Act.

Prior to 1963 it seems to have been assumed that 'first come, first served' was the operating maxim, but historical precedent alone could not maintain the supplies of long-established abstractors if new abstractors became active upstream, or alongside in the same aquifer.

Two innovations of the Water Resources Act 1963 are important in this context. Firstly, the Act required that all abstractions, old and new, from surface and underground sources, be licensed, that is authorised by the River Authority and limited in quantity and rate of withdrawal. Secondly, abstracted water was no longer a free commodity. Each abstractor paid a small fee for his licence (since abolished by the Water Act 1973) and then a charge for the water, calculated according to the licensed quantity and various criteria of source, season and use.

Yet neither a licence to take an authorised quantity of water for spray irrigation nor the appropriate payment can guarantee that water. It can only be taken if it is available. In a severe drought or other emergency a temporary restriction may be imposed, under section 45 of the 1963 Act denying water altogether or reducing the amount to be taken. The balance of water supply and demand in south east England is such that when drought occurs the demand for spray irrigation cannot be met in full. The 1976 drought was exceptionally severe and many groups besides the spray irrigators were forced to reduce their water consumption. More significant in the long term are the more frequent, lesser droughts – such as that in East Anglia in the summer of 1973 – which inconvenience no other consumers but nonetheless impose restrictions on irrigators. Other consumers are affected only after the enactment of special drought legislation (the Drought Act 1976, for instance): irrigators' supplies are vulnerable in less extreme conditions and without the invocation of special powers.

The irrigated area in the south eastern counties might expand greatly if water were plentiful and cheap. In the Great Ouse basin as much as 40 percent of the total area might benefit from irrigation (Ministry of Housing and Local Government 1960: 8). Certainly there is a very large 'theoretical' demand for irrigation water, calculated as the difference between the crops' requirements in their growing seasons and the available soil moisture. But it is equally certain that irrigation development will be cut short well before it reaches this point, by the limits on available water on the one hand, by the economics of management of individual farms on the other, and by the licensing and charging policies of the Water Authorities which in practice link the two.

Abstraction licensing

The Water Resources Act required that all except the very smallest abstractions be licensed, and the licensing scheme came into operation in 1965. Those abstractors who had been taking water regularly during the preceding five years were granted 'licences of right' in acknowledgement of their historic claims upon the resource. A licence of right was indeed a right – it could not be refused an established abstractor, it was issued without limit of time, and in general the quantities authorised for abstraction were equivalent to those taken in the past. Licences of right thus put a seal of approval upon the allocation pattern as it was before 1965.

Would-be new abstractors have to apply for an 'ordinary' licence, which the Water Authority is at liberty to refuse altogether, grant subject to a reduction in the quantity to be taken, or grant subject to a time limit. The distinction between the two types of licence is therefore an important one for the degree of Water Authority control. As the aim of the licensing scheme is to ensure that abstractions do not over-strain the river system at any time, new abstractions can be authorised only if there is surplus water, over and above the needs of in-stream users and of existing legitimate abstractors.

Over 1500 licences for spray irrigation purposes have been issued for the Great Ouse basin, over 80 percent of them issued in the first two years, and all but a handful being licences of right. An increasing number of ordinary licences have been granted recently, and particularly in the first half of 1976, reflecting a continuing demand from spray irrigators, but still the bulk of the licences and of the water authorised for abstraction belongs to the irrigators operating before 1965.

The Ministry of Agriculture's periodic surveys of irrigation show that in England and Wales there has been a decline in the irrigated area after a peak in 1965 (figure 13). The 1963 Act's licensing and charging schemes must be partly responsible, together with tighter controls on capital available for irrigation systems. In the Great Ouse basin not all the licences issued are now in force. Some farmers have changed their agricultural practice and abandoned irrigation altogether or have used fewer abstraction points. In 1974 there were just under 1000 spray irrigation licences in force, of which all but 192 were licences of right. Of the quantities authorised for abstraction, two thirds are from surface and one third from underground sources.

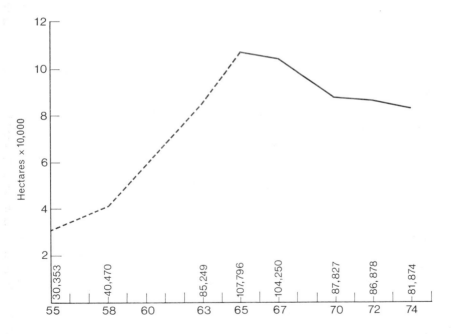

Figure 13   Total area irrigated in a dry season.
Source: Information from the Ministry of Agriculture, Fisheries and Food.

The present authorised abstraction for spray irrigation is about one third less than formerly, a reduction due in part to the revision of some of the original licences of right. In essence the case is simple and near universal. When water is to be had for the taking, the demand is greater than when it must be applied for and paid for. In the early days of the licensing scheme the Great Ouse River Authority was having to deal with so many licence of right applications that close investigation was impossible. It was suspected that many irrigators were exaggerating the quantities abstracted in the past, in the hope of securing a future supply adequate for conditions of extreme drought, but these suspected excesses could not be confirmed. More than a few came to light when abstraction charges were imposed in 1969. Farmers were reluctant to pay for water they rarely or never used. As they saw the financial implications, many of them requested the River Authority to reduce the authorised quantities and thus the charge, an adjustment willingly made in order to release the water for other users.

Once the licences of right were issued, each River Authority had to decide whether new abstractions could be accommodated. Licensing control itself helped in this process by providing new information about the demands being made on present supplies. Before the 1963 Act the abstractions of the statutory water undertakers were known in some detail, but both large and small uncontrolled abstractions took place, probably in total withdrawing more water than the water undertakers, and about which almost nothing was known.

To make the allocation task for river abstraction easier, the Water Resources Act advanced the idea of 'minimum acceptable flow', the river flow needed for legitimate in-stream and abstractive uses. This central concept of the legislation was defined in section 19 as 'not less than the minimum which in the opinion of the river authority is needed for safeguarding the public health and for meeting (in respect of both quantity and quality of water) the requirements of existing lawful uses of the inland water'. River flows in excess of the minimum acceptable could be considered surplus to present needs and allocated for new abstractions.

The Act suggested that each River Authority would set minimum acceptable flows at various significant points within its area and judge applications for new licences against them. In the event no minimum acceptable flows were set for the Great Ouse, and the concept has now been abandoned everywhere. Early definition was difficult because streamflow records often covered only a short period and did not indicate much of the natural range of flow fluctuations. Of course with time this problem has lessened, but it was an initial obstacle. Then, while the Act presented minimum acceptable flow as a fixed quantity, several hydrologists argued that the flow should vary throughout the year to take account of variable seasonal demand, for example from migratory fish (Boulton 1965 and discussion following). Another difficulty was keeping formally defined flows up to date, as flow conditions and demands on the river changed. Finally the River Authorities were concerned that on some of their rivers the summertime dry weather flow might be considerably below the minimum acceptable, and that a formal definition which exposed this deficiency might upset public confidence.

The essential criteria for deciding whether or not to allow a new abstraction remain the overall effects upon the resource – what will be left, in quantity and quality, for other users. Season of abstraction must be considered for surface sources, summer abstractions such as those for spray irrigation having greater depletion effects. Another set of relevant factors is the proportion of abstracted water to be returned to the system, the point of return in relation to the point of abstraction, and the quality of the returned water. And here again spray irrigation has a profound effect, with very little water being returned. Abstraction for spray irrigation is assumed to be a 100 percent loss to the system in the Great Ouse. As a result there is no direct problem with water quality. Spray irrigation is not a polluter, except in a most general way in aiding the percolation of agricultural chemicals into rivers and aquifers. However, totally consumptive abstractions reduce the amount of relatively clean water available to dilute incoming effluents. This, with its associated amenity effects, has been a limiting factor on new irrigation abstractions in parts of the Great Ouse basin.

The River Ivel, a tributary of the Great Ouse, gives an example. During average summer conditions 50 percent of the flow in the river is effluent. In the dry spring and summer months of 1973 irrigation abstractors took out so much water that there were then two parts of effluent to one part of clean water. Additional summer abstractions cannot be tolerated if the Ivel is to continue to receive effluent without being offensive to sight and smell. No new licences for spray irrigation are being issued for the Ivel basin, unless water is withdrawn in the winter and stored over-season.

The Water Authorities are able to regulate new abstractions very finely. Applications for abstractions may be refused; the quantities authorised for withdrawal may be reduced from the original applications; and the licences may be issued for a specific period of time. Many of the Great Ouse's spray irrigation licences are for periods of five years only. The general expectation – and it is no more than an expectation – is that another licence will be issued at the end of the period, allowing the irrigator to continue, but this short-term method gives the Water Authority flexibility to change quantities, season of abstraction and even source of water as circumstances demand.

There is no such flexibility with licences of right. The Water Resources Act assumed that if an abstraction was already taking place, it could be supported in the future. The water must have been there to take, and it would continue to be there unless appropriated by newcomers. However, the Water Authorities are not compelled to meet all licences of right. New licences must be honoured, but licences of right do not have to be, a necessary protection for the Authorities in the obvious case of abstraction from ephemeral streams and the less obvious case of spray irrigation.

Where the abstraction has a fixed pattern, for example a constant daily withdrawal or a peak summer / low winter withdrawal with much the same amplitude of fluctuation year after year, the licence of right probably can and should be met, but spray irrigation abstractions are different in nature. Crop requirements for water in the growing periods vary from one crop year to the next according to rainfall and the factors controlling evaporation. For cultivation in the open, irrigation is supplementary to rainfall, in contrast to irrigation in arid areas or to watering in greenhouses where the artificial application of water is essential to plant growth. The aim of supplemental irrigation is to make up the soil moisture deficit, a highly variable parameter. The exaggerations already noted in the licence of right applications, some intentional, some unintentional no doubt, resulted from the farmers' desires to procure sufficient water to meet their crops' needs in extremely dry conditions. Such conditions might not arise more than one year in twenty, perhaps more rarely still but, with the spectre of water 'rationing' near, many farmers thought it worth applying for enough water to meet so unlikely an event. Many new irrigation schemes are designed to meet water requirements in the fifth driest year in twenty, but hundreds of licences of right in the Great Ouse catchment authorise abstractions adequate for much rarer droughts.

The fundamental question is whether these authorised quantities can actually be taken from rivers and aquifers, should conditions warrant it. In many sections of the Great Ouse, the answer is negative, as the 1976 drought demonstrated so clearly. On the River Ivel the quantities authorised for spray irrigation come very close to the actual summer flows. The maximum permitted abstraction would cause the river to dry up. In the last five irrigation seasons up to 1976 the water taken for spray irrigation in the Great Ouse basin has been rather less than 25 percent of the authorised seasonal quantity. A survey of the Ivel basin, conducted by the River Authority during the irrigation peak of 1973, suggested that the daily abstractions, which are more meaningful in terms of fluctuations in river flow, were no more than 40 percent of the daily authorised quantities.

Section 45 of the Water Resources Act 1963 enables the Water Authorities to impose temporary restrictions on irrigation withdrawals in time of water shortage. In fact these powers have not been invoked in the Great Ouse basin, even during 1976, but abstractions have been reduced through the 'voluntary restraint' of irrigators who understand that section 45 powers will be used if they do not cooperate. Farmers value the freedom to manage their own supply reductions, devising crop patterns and irrigation regimes to match. Voluntary restraint, agreed with the National Farmers Union, has worked well in that irrigators have achieved the reductions required by the Water Authority, but this is at the cost of leaving expensive equipment unused and losing agricultural production.

Charges for abstracted water: present policies and some possible alternatives

Along with licensing control, the Water Resources Act 1963 introduced the general principle that abstractors should pay for their water, and in April 1969 the River Authorities' charging schemes came into operation. The Great Ouse River Authority had made fair progress in devising its particular method of charging, and this came to serve as a model for several others in the country. From 1969 onwards the water allocation process was not solely an administrative one. The schedules of water charges were designed to defray the costs of resource conservation and development, and there was no deliberate attempt to use water charges as a regulator of demand. Nonetheless, since cost is rarely irrelevant to an abstractor, the charging schemes must have influenced the application for licences and the resulting allocation, even if the influence has been rather diffuse.

A central government memorandum in 1967 (Ministry of Housing and Local Government and Welsh Office) advised the River Authorities on the structure of the charging schemes, and in 1969 each authority published its own detailed schedule. Following the reorganisation of the water industry and the new powers for levying charges for water services (Water Act 1973: sections 30–1), the National Water Council issued a memorandum on abstraction charges (National Water Council 1976: appendix V) reiterating much of the 1967 advice but stressing that the regional application of the broad principles must be a matter for each Water Authority to decide for itself.

The charging schemes for abstracted water developed by the River Authorities, and in most cases continued by the Water Authorities, were based on three principles. First, the charges levied were in aggregate to meet the costs of providing water and developing the resources in the Authority's area. River Authorities fixed charges to cover expenditure on their water resources accounts, which included hydrometric schemes and conservation works.

Secondly the charges levied were to be based on the quantities authorised for abstraction, not on the quantities actually taken, with the partial exception of spray irrigation. With licence inspectors to enforce the controls, there is little opportunity for an abstractor to take very much more than his permitted amount. Often he will take less, but he is required to pay the full charge because, it is argued, that water has been safeguarded for him and any other method would make it difficult for the authority to calculate its expected revenue in any year. Thus the abstractor cannot reduce his water bill by economising on water use and there is no financial incentive to reduce waste. Only if the licence is altered to reduce the authorised quantity does the abstractor see any benefit from economising on water use.

Spray irrigation is an exception to this general rule. To charge irrigators on the full authorised quantities every year would be unfair in view of the fact that the abstractions may be restricted under the 1963 Act. Yet to charge on the water actually taken would not only place irrigators at a distinct advantage compared with other users but would deny the water agencies proper reimbursement for conserving water in case of high irrigation demand in any particular year. The agreed compromise was to charge on a two-part tariff, one part referring to the authorised quantity and the other to the abstracted quantity. Thus an irrigator taking less than his authorised quantity pays *less* than if charged normally but *more* than if charged just for the abstracted quantity.

The third principle of the charging schemes was that the costs to be covered were to be shared among licence holders in proportion to the effect of their abstractions upon the resource. This division takes account of source of water, season of abstraction, and use to which the water is put, as this affects the quantity and quality of water returned to the system.

The charging scheme applied by the Great Ouse River Authority, and continued by the Anglian Water Authority, considered the effects upon the resource as follows:

Characteristics of the source. Except in relation to season, there should be no difference between surface and groundwater abstractions. Nor should there be any difference between water taken from different parts of the catchment, saving the case of saline water, chargeable at one tenth the rate for fresh water.

Season of the year. Season was thought to be unimportant for groundwater abstractions, so that one rate is applied throughout the year. Surface abstractions are differentiated: winter 1, annual 2, and summer 4. All groundwater abstractions and annual (all year round) surface abstractions are rated similarly, with winter surface abstractions at half and summer surface abstractions at double this rate.

Purpose or use. Here the differences are based on two considerations: loss of quantity and loss of quality. For loss of quantity the percentage losses assumed are:

industrial cooling	loss	2 percent
raw vegetable washing		5
public water supply and industry		20
spray irrigation		100

Loss of quality was thought to be significant where water is used for raw vegetable washing, for public supply and for industry.

The current charges (1976–7) in the Great Ouse Division of the Anglian Water Authority show the effects of this classification. The typical spray irrigation charge, for summer abstraction from a river, is a fraction under £42.00 per million gallons.* For winter surface abstractions taken into storage the charge is £10.50 per million gallons. The charge for all year abstractions for public supply and industry is £5.25 per million gallons, the difference accounted for partly by the seasonal patterns of abstraction but mainly by the different rates of water loss in these uses.

The rationale for the charging schemes is clearly stated, that the costs of works for water conservation and development be defrayed among different categories of abstractor according to their effects upon the resource. But this is an unusual way of charging for a commodity. The normal market determinants of price here give way to non-economic determinants – effects upon the resource – which only the Water Authorities can assess. The water charges are determined internally, and there is nothing against which to judge their 'correctness', apart from the facts that in aggregate they cover costs and that they are accepted by the purchasing public.

An alternative method of charging is to relate individual charges to the actual costs of providing the water, but this was specifically ruled out for the charging schemes. The 1967 memorandum of advice stated that 'the cost of conservation projects should be defrayed on a common basis throughout the authority's area. Established abstractors should not therefore be regarded as excluded from liability to bear a share of the cost of new conservation works simply on the ground that their abstractions can be maintained without such works' (Ministry of Housing and Local Government and Welsh Office 1967: 2). The recent National Water Council memorandum made the same point, that while the early abstractors have protection against later licence applications which might affect their rights, they are not entitled to preferential treatment where charges are concerned. Aggregate costs, not individual costs are relevant: early appropriation of a cheap supply does not protect an abstractor against later charges for the development of new and more expensive supplies for the benefit of other users.

In favour of charging the costs of individual resource projects directly to their beneficiaries one can note the brake this exercises on excess expenditure. In theory at least each project is developed only if the potential beneficiaries are prepared to pay for the water so provided. Benefits are seen to justify costs, and benefits and costs fall on the same people. In considering aggregate costs only the chosen method puts old and new abstractors on the same footing as regards water costs, but loses thereby a simple check that each project is economically worth while.

* 1 million gallons = 4.546 Ml.

Another possibility is to consider charges in relation to the value of water in use. 'Value in use' can be taken as the value added to a single product, a group of products or the gross output of a region by the application of a unit of water. When the cost of water is set close to its value in use, water users are encouraged to reduce waste, that is to purchase only the amount of water they will use productively, and even to substitute other factors of production, for instance by changing an industrial process so that less water is needed or by applying more fertiliser instead of water to agricultural land. Wollman (1962), in a study of the value of water in alternative uses in New Mexico, showed that the productivity of water when used for manufacturing, processing raw materials and public supply was very much higher than when used for agriculture. In the absence of evidence to the contrary, one might assume that the patterns of variation of value in use in Britain are roughly similar. If so, one might expect water to be used for irrigation only if it were comparatively cheap, while other uses could afford water at much higher prices. That irrigators in the Great Ouse basin are still eager for water at the maximum rate of £42 per million gallons suggests that the whole charging schedule is setting charges well below water's value in different uses.

In theory resources are allocated efficiently when all users derive equal value from the last or marginal unit of water they take (the principle known as equimarginal value in use). For such an allocation to be achieved, one of two conditions must obtain. Either it must be possible to buy and sell water rights without restriction, their market value then settling at and measuring the marginal value in use. Or alternatively, if a water agency sells water, the marginal price must be set equal to marginal cost for all customers. The costs of providing water vary according to the location of the customer and the type of service he is given.

The principles of marginal cost charging are far easier to state than to apply in practice. Trading of water rights to establish their market value is impossible in this country. Under the alternative system of sale of water by a water agency, it is unlikely that all quota restrictions – authorised quantities – will be abolished to allow demand to be controlled solely by price. And then it may be very difficult to determine in particular cases what the marginal costs of the system really are. Marginal cost charging, even in a hybrid form with the Water Authorities retaining some direct control over quantities of water abstracted, would be most difficult to implement in the near future. The Committee on Economic and Financial Policies in the Water Industry advanced marginal cost charging as a means of promoting the efficient use of resources, but did not expect its early or widespread adoption because of present limited knowledge of marginal costs (Department of the Environment 1974b: 32–6).

After considering some alternative methods of charging, we can see how far from economic efficiency is the method presently used, with charges levied on licensed rather than abstracted quantities, with variations according to category of use, in reverse order to the water's value in use, but always well below that value. Yet the point must not be laboured: efficiency in water allocation is not a goal pursued through the charging schemes. In fact, though termed abstraction charges, the charges levied are not purely for abstraction. They contain an element of water use, since the return of water is also taken into account. Spray irrigation charges are as high as they are because almost no water is returned. Less consumptive uses are charged less, being credited for the returned water. The charging schemes hold back from a full consideration of water use, however, ignoring effluent disposal. The result is that the charging schemes are well nigh impossible to justify in economic terms, since they levy neither water use charges nor abstraction charges in the strict sense.

Nonetheless the charges seem reasonable to most water abstractors. Before the introduction of the charging schemes, public inquiries were held where there was opposition to the proposals, but in the Great Ouse basin only very minor changes were thought necessary. In general the schemes' hydrologic basis are well accepted by the public (if not necessarily well understood), and the charges paid cover expenditure. Alternative methods could perhaps do away with the need for administrative allocation, ensure that each water resource project is economically justified, or reduce waste in water use. The charging schemes do none of these things themselves. Their aims are simple and limited, leaving the more difficult tasks to be tackled elsewhere.

Supply and demand for irrigation water

Farmers' requests for irrigation water in part determine the Water Authorities' allocation through licensing and are themselves in part determined by the licensing and charging policies. There is no doubt that in the Great Ouse basin, one of the driest in Britain, rainfall is frequently insufficient to maintain maximum plant growth and that more reliable, better quality and earlier maturing crops can be achieved by supplemental irrigation.

Not all the crops commonly grown in the Great Ouse basin would benefit from irrigation, but totalling the areas of those crops which would, in East Anglian conditions, do significantly better with irrigation produced the alarming figure of 840 000 acres (340 000 hectares), or about 40 percent of the area of the basin (Ministry of Housing and Local Government 1960). The water needed to sustain this area is not available in the catchment: resources are already taxed by the present irrigated area, estimated to be less than 50 000 acres (20 000 hectares).

Such an estimate of potential irrigation demand, which translates into a seasonal water requirement of 150 000 million gallons (682 000 Ml), ignores all considerations of water cost and availability, and is obviously no measure of the practical demand which the Water Authority must take into account in planning future resource development and allocation.

Since 1960 four major reports have wrestled with the problem of forecasting the 'real' demand for irrigation water in the Great Ouse basin. The Natural Resources (Technical) Committee (Office of the Minister of Science 1962) put the practical limit of demand at 130 000 acres (53 000 hectares), but the report of Binnie and Partners (Ministry of Housing and Local Government 1965) suggested that growth towards this ceiling would be checked short by availability of water at a suitable price, and put the likely figure for the year 2000 at around 75 000 acres (30 000 hectares). Such an area might require 10 000 million gallons of water (45 500 Ml) in a year of peak demand, with the summer demand reaching 100 million gallons (455 Ml) a day. The Water Resources Board (1966a) forecast much more substantial increases in the irrigated area and water demand by the turn of the century, with an acreage of 121 000 (49 000 hectares) demanding around 14 000 million gallons (63 600 Ml) in a peak year and as much as 219 million gallons (1000 Ml) on a peak irrigation day. These figures come close to the ceiling suggested by the Natural Resources (Technical) Committee. The Great Ouse River Authority (unpublished survey 1974) introduced another estimate for the year 2001, the lowest figure yet, 6000 million gallons (27 000 Ml) a year.

The four investigations used different bases for forecasting demand. The Natural Resources (Technical) Committee gave a practical limit based on assumptions that, with little change in the general pattern of farming, a third of the vegetable area, a third of the farm crop area and half an acre of grassland per dairy cow would be irrigated, to meet the water deficit in eight years out of ten. The Great Ouse River Authority study extrapolated past growth in the quantities licensed for abstraction, and the other two reports distinguished two types of irrigation with different growth rates – Binnie and Partners separating summer- and winter-stored abstractions, and the Water Resources Board (1966a) separating irrigation of high and low value crops. In these circumstances it would be remarkable indeed if the results of the calculations were the same, but such very widely varying estimates lead one to doubt whether it is worth while to attempt a forecast at all.

Certainly *Water Resources in England and Wales* gave no detailed forecasts of 'such an intermittent and unpredictable demand' (Water Resources Board 1973a vol 1: 34), though it considered public supply and industrial demands at some length. The Water Resources Board assumed, as did the Natural Resources (Technical) Committee also, that any future demand for spray irrigation, beyond that which can be supplied from spare summer flows, would be met from irrigators' own storage and not from new strategic storage.

The assumption that the costs of new irrigation supplies should be private rather than public is in reality an important policy decision. It is based on the argument that overall it is cheaper for storage to be provided by the irrigators themselves than for part of the yield of public development works to be reserved for such a highly variable demand. Yet the costs of storage falling on the individual farmer may make his water much more expensive than if he had abstracted it direct and paid the maximum summer charge, as the example below shows. In most cases there is no financial incentive to provide over-season storage: the difference between summer and winter abstraction charges is not great enough to compensate for the costs of construction. Of course, storage may be forced on the farmer who is refused a summer abstraction licence but who still wants to irrigate. There is also a more subtle encouragement to storage, in the securer supply it gives. In times of severe drought when direct abstractions for irrigation are reduced or cut off altogether, it is only the farmer with over-season storage who can continue to irrigate on a large scale. His profits in the market are magnified as a result of his neighbours' lost or damaged crops. But the benefits of security are too subtle, or too meagre in relation to costs to influence all irrigators, and in the Great Ouse basin there is still insufficient private storage to maintain the irrigated area through a moderate drought, let alone through a very severe one.

To show the differing economic circumstances of irrigators making direct summer abstractions from rivers and those using winter storage, let us compare two hypothetical examples (table 1). Two similar farms are assumed, irrigating about 40 acres, with a dry season demand for water of around 4 million gallons.* They face the same costs for pumps, mains and field equipment, but the water charges are different under the charging scheme, being £42.00 per million gallons for the summer-abstracting farm and only £10.50 per million gallons for the winter abstractor. (For the sake of simplicity the two-part tariff is ignored here.) The winter abstractor has to build a reservoir to hold rather more than 4 million gallons of water over-season, since around 10 percent of the stored water may be lost through evaporation and seepage. If annual costs are calculated over a period of ten years and it is assumed that the interest rate is 15 percent, we find that the winter abstractor has to pay over £612 a year more for his irrigation supply.

After ten years, having paid for his reservoir, the winter abstractor saves about £31.50 a year in water charges, and at this rate it would take well over a century for the winter abstractor to recoup his reservoir costs from the saving in water charges. Capital costs and interest charges are so high compared with water charges that the differential rates for winter and summer abstractions have little effect on the final calculation.

The high cost of over-season storage has implications for the type of crops to be grown. The financial returns per unit of water applied vary markedly from crop to crop. High value crops such as celery, cauliflower, peas, lettuce and other market garden produce, and early and main crop potatoes give the farmer good returns and may justify even an expensive storage scheme. Grass for dairy cattle, on the other hand, does not seem to justify storage.

*Imperial units are used here because water charges are still levied on quantities measured in gallons.

TABLE 1   *Comparison of annual irrigation costs with summer- and winter-stored abstraction*

	£	£
Common costs of pump, mains and mobile irrigation equipment, after deduction of 20 percent farm capital grant,		
per acre	172*	
For 40 acres	6880	
Annual equivalent of capital assuming recoupment over 10 years and interest at 15 percent		1370
Annual repairs		200
Total common costs		1570
Farm 1: *Direct summer abstraction*		
Common costs		1570
Water charges: 4 million gallons at £42.00 per million		168
Total annual costs (excluding labour)		1738
Farm 2: *Winter-stored abstraction*		
Common costs		1570
Water charges: 4 million gallons at £10.50 per million		42
Construction costs of reservoir to store 4 million gallons, at £1000 per million,** after deduction of 20 percent grant	3200	
Annual equivalent of capital		638
Annual repairs		100
Total annual costs (excluding labour)		2350
Difference in annual costs		612

* Figures from C N Prickett, MAFF, private communication.
** Based on recent costs of construction in East Anglia.

Sugar beet, too, was a marginal crop for irrigation, but recent increases in beet prices have increased its irrigation chances.

The economics of irrigation vary from farm to farm and from year to year, and no ready and convincing answer can be given to the question of how far on-farm winter storage will provide for irrigation needs. Informed opinion has differed. Binnie and Partners (Ministry of Housing and Local Government 1965) thought that a large increase in the area supplied from storage was unlikely, and estimated that less than 20 percent of the Great Ouse's irrigation use in the year 2000 would be storage-supplied. Prickett (1966: 453), referring to the whole country, considered winter storage to be the main prospect for irrigation supply, the south east of the country having the greatest need for winter storage. The extent to which these predictions are realised depends also upon Water Authority policy. The Anglian Water Authority, heavily over-committed to irrigators' licences of right, is cautious about issuing further licences for unsupported summer abstractions and is encouraging the construction of on-farm storage to a degree probably not foreseen by Binnie and Partners.

In future one might expect an increasing volume of water to be taken for irrigation, but with a greater proportion taken in the winter, and used on the same or even a smaller irrigated area. Already the irrigated area has decreased since 1965, and irrigation of the lower value crops such as grass and sugar beet has contracted quite markedly. A further concentration on high value crops seems inevitable, given rising costs of equipment and storage, and apart from potatoes the highest value crops tend to cover small areas. Even where the same crops continue to be irrigated, there is a discernible trend to use rather more water to maintain high yielding, high quality crops on a smaller area.

Priorities in water allocation

Spray irrigation is no longer the run-away water demand it was feared to be in the early 1960s. Irrigation expansion has come to a halt in certain parts of East Anglia, where it is incompatible with other higher priority water uses. It has been taken for granted by water planners in Britain that domestic requirements have highest priority, but the Natural Resources (Technical) Committee (Office of the Minister of Science 1962) advanced arguments for considering the supply of water for irrigation alongside that for industry, after domestic requirements had been met. In practice this has not come about: irrigation is not ranked equally with industry. Irrigators are the only group of abstractors commonly given only short-term licences and they are the only group whose supplies can be cut off or reduced by the Water Authority without recourse to special drought legislation.

The reasons for the low priority given to irrigation use can be found both in social preference and in the effects upon the physical resource. To many people supplemental irrigation still appears a luxury, admittedly increasing agricultural output and farmers' income, but neither improving local employment opportunities nor changing the economic structure of the region, as an additional allocation of water to industry might do. The nature of the demand also forces irrigation into its low position on the list: other less intense and less consumptive abstractions are necessarily viewed more favourably.

For these same reasons the burden of providing over-season storage of water for irrigation falls on the farmers themselves. Here again irrigation is at variance with other abstractive uses for which water is supplied from public resource developments. Irrigation farmers pay more for their water than any other group of abstractors, bearing the highest of the charges imposed by the Water Authorities, with the addition, in an increasing number of cases, of the costs of over-season storage. The fear that irrigators might pirate the supplies of other water users is groundless now, although this was a real possibility before the Water Resources Act. The Act's licensing and charging schemes have together deterred many would-be irrigators, and it is surely no accident that the most recent estimate of future irrigation demand in the Great Ouse basin (Great Ouse River Authority, in draft form, 1974) is also the lowest.

The allocation procedure is effective in restricting the quantities of water going to the irrigators, but two questions remain to be discussed: has the Act operated in the manner intended; and is the resulting allocation a fair one?

The concept of minimum acceptable flow, incorporated in the Act to assist allocation decisions, was early cast aside and in this respect the Act has not functioned according to the original design. If as some hydrologists have argued minimum acceptable flow is an unworkable sophistication, its loss is not to be regretted.

The intention of the licence of right clauses was to safeguard existing patterns of water use, giving them priority over new or increased uses. The justice of this is not beyond question, but the alternative – the periodic comparison of existing and potential uses on an equal basis with, where necessary, adjustments in existing uses – was never a real contender in the political sphere. The essential point here is that in the case of spray irrigation some wrong acknowledgments were made and cannot now be corrected. O'Riordan (1970) noted that the East Suffolk and Norfolk River Authority (now also part of the Anglian Water Authority) was over-committed to irrigators' licences of right, though the quantities licensed had sometimes been substantially reduced from the quantities applied for. Likewise in the Great Ouse basin too much water was granted to the licence of right irrigators, and less than a quarter of this has actually been used in recent irrigation seasons. In practice irrigation abstractions are controlled not by licences but by temporary voluntary restrictions. The section 45 powers to restrict abstraction have not been used, but without them in reserve voluntary restraint would probably have been far less effective. If temporary restrictions, voluntary or otherwise, intended for emergency use in times of severe drought, come to be used as a matter of course, then the licences themselves are irrelevant.

By methods rather different from those outlined in the Water Resources Act, an allocation of water is effected and competing uses are accommodated. The allocation pattern is accepted by the water users, but other allocations might also be acceptable – and preferable to certain interests. Many spray irrigators feel they are treated unfairly in comparison with industrial water users, and both irrigators and industrial users point to over-allocation and waste in domestic water supply.

Beneath the present arrangements lie the social preferences which accord established use priority over new use and public water supply priority over the others. Other preferences might give other allocation patterns, and we may already have witnessed some reordering of preferences as an immediate response to the 1976 drought. In the area most acutely affected, south east Wales, domestic consumption was very severely restricted to save water for industry and so delay disruption of production and employment. In East Anglia crops withered away while irrigation equipment stood idle, and in neither area did any over-allocation of water for domestic use go unchallenged. Indeed, as the drought intensified over the whole country, domestic supply yielded its position to industry and agriculture. How far this is merely a short-term change it is hard to say. The spray irrigation clauses of the Water Resources Act 1963 were in part at least a response to the 1959 drought. The considered response to the 1976 drought might well be to find these clauses unduly restrictive and to afford spray irrigation rather more favourable treatment in the future.

CHAPTER 5

THE MANAGEMENT OF GROUNDWATER RESOURCES

Groundwater has been a source of local supply from very early times, but during the last century the Chalk and Triassic Sandstone aquifers of south, central and east England became important regional sources where growing water demand coincided with comparatively meagre surface flows. Today about a quarter of the water supply of England and Wales comes from groundwater, if cooling water cycling is excluded, and in the Great Ouse basin, dry above but with several water-bearing rocks beneath, a third of the licensed abstraction is from groundwater.

Groundwater is invisible until it is pumped up, and there are no simple means of determining how much water is stored below ground or how quickly any withdrawal for supply is made good by rainfall percolating to recharge the aquifers. Earlier use of groundwater often led to rapid local lowering of water levels, increased pumping costs and even the drying up of wells, with the additional problem in areas near the sea of intrusion of saline water to contaminate the freshwater supply. The aquifers below London give a striking illustration of the difficulties of managing the underground resource.

At the beginning of the eighteenth century the water-bearing Tertiary Sands beneath the London Clay were tapped for the first time by deep wells at Paddington and Kilburn. The Industrial Revolution stimulated further well construction and in 1823 the Chalk aquifer below the Tertiaries was penetrated at Chiswick and Hammersmith. From then on well construction developed rapidly, as figure 14 shows reaching peaks of over forty wells a year during the period 1908 to 1937. The two World Wars and years of acute industrial depression interrupted constructional activity, and since 1945 a system of licensing has checked further development of the aquifers.

The effects of this abstraction are shown in the maps of groundwater contours (figure 15). Up to 1950 there was, over the London Basin as a whole, a continual lowering of water levels, necessitating the deepening of existing wells which, nevertheless, tended to yield less water than before. Saline water was drawn into the aquifers in areas close to the Thames estuary. The London Clay settled slightly as water leaked down into the dewatered rocks beneath, and this caused subsidence, greatest where the dewatering effect was greatest. The flow of rivers draining the outcrop areas of the Tertiaries and Chalk was reduced as the groundwater component of the flow decreased.

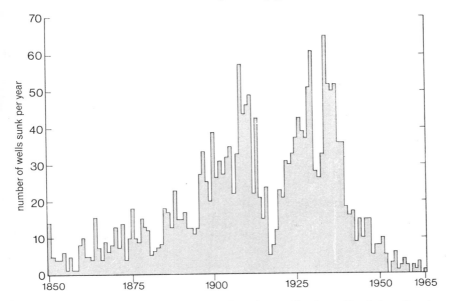

Figure 14   Construction of wells tapping the confined aquifer below London 1850–1965.
Source: Water Resources Board 1972a:15.

Concern at these manifestations of over-development led to the restriction of new groundwater withdrawals, following the Water Act 1945. Furthermore, many wells were, by this time, out of service, either because of war damage or because water levels had fallen to depths from which it was no longer economic to pump. These factors combined to reduce abstractions and hold them at a lower level, so that by 1965 the fall of groundwater contours had been arrested in west and central London. In the eastern part of the London Basin, and particularly north of the Thames, the decline continues, though at a slower rate.

If over-exploitation is to be avoided, it is necessary to calculate the safe yield of an aquifer – the quantity of water that can be withdrawn for supply without cumulative depletion – and to control abstraction at or below the safe yield. What is taken out must, in the long term, be made up by recharge, with the volume of storage and the rate of movement of water in the aquifer determining the permissible short-term deviations from the equilibrium. The basic groundwater equation

inflow (or recharge) = outflow (or discharge) ± change in storage

may involve several different inflows and outflows. The principal inflow is rainfall percolation from the outcrop area, but in addition there may be natural recharge through a river or lake bed, and two forms of man-assisted

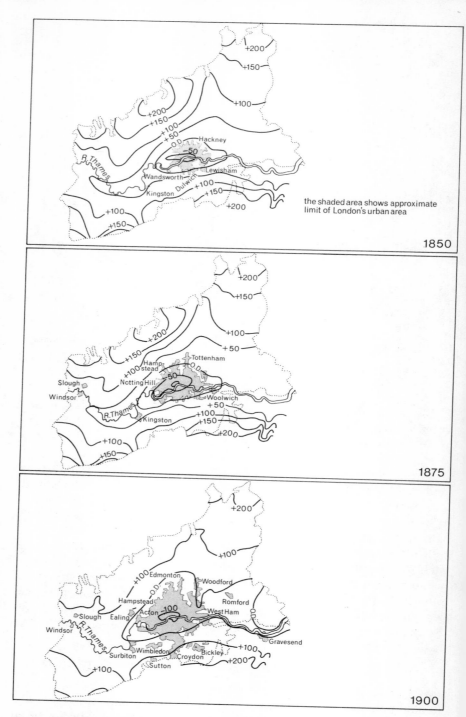

Figure 15 Groundwater contours in the London Basin 1850–1965.

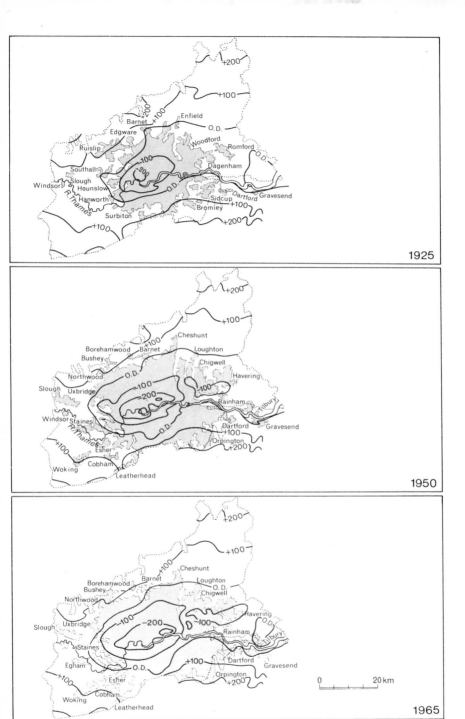

Based on Water Resources Board 1972a: plate V.

recharge, one accidental from excessive irrigation or leakage from water mains, and the other intentional, artificial recharge. The principal outflows are the natural groundwater component of river flow (the sole component in dry weather), leakages to other aquifers and to the sea, and abstractions by man. When the variables have been identified and measured, the sign of the 'change in storage' term indicates whether resources are available for development or whether the aquifer is in deficit.

Ground and surface waters are inter-linked in the hydrologic system, as figures 2 and 3 (pp. 5–6) have shown, with a flow of river water into the underlying aquifer at some times of the year and a flow of groundwater into the river at others. Former use of ground and surface waters tended to develop them separately, without reference to each other, but recently the water management system has copied the hydrologic system in considering the resources together.

A first stage in the integration of ground and surface waters is their alternating or 'conjunctive' use. Traditionally consumers have used either river or groundwater for direct, continuous supply, or perhaps both together in fixed quantities. Conjunctive use gives greater flexibility, with the supply system drawing on surface sources when they are abundant and then switching to pump groundwater as river levels fall. In theory at any one time the supply may come entirely from one source, entirely from the other, or be made up of any mixture of the two. The benefit is an overall contribution to supply substantially greater than the combined yields of the two resources managed separately.

Groundwater augmentation of river flows is a second stage of integrated development, and is in essence an extension of the natural process whereby the aquifer provides the dry weather flow of the river. The aim of river regulation is to maintain flows above the natural minimum so that abstractions and in-stream uses can continue downstream: an addition of groundwater is one way of achieving this. When river flows are low, boreholes are pumped and the water transferred to the watercourse, the dewatered aquifer being left to recharge normally during rainy periods. The benefits of this type of integration of sources are that many uses and reuses of the additional water are possible, while the water has been provided more cheaply and more conveniently from the aquifer than from new surface storage.

A third stage of integrated development is the artificial recharge of the aquifer, when there is empty storage space below ground and surplus water above. Surface water is transferred to the dewatered rock, usually through wells or basins, and stored there to be pumped out later. Past over-pumping has unintentionally created storage space in several of the major aquifers, space which may be used as an alternative to surface storage.

Figure 16 indicates how integration of surface and underground sources can increase the yield of the system. When a river source is used on its own, development is limited by the dry weather flow (which may have already

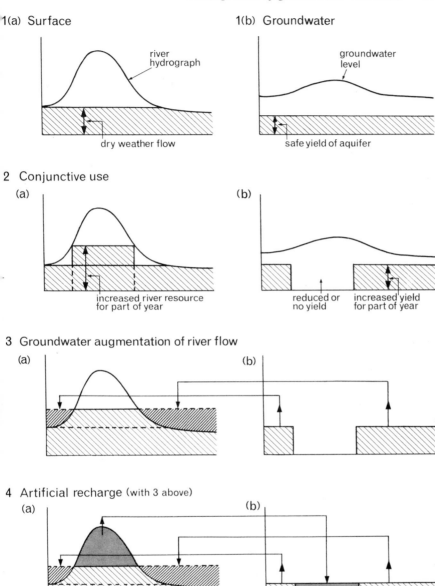

Figure 16   Integration of surface and groundwater resources.

been increased above the natural minimum by releases from surface storage). When an underground source is used continuously on its own, its development is limited to the natural safe yield (1a and b). With conjunctive use (2a and b) exploitation of the river source can be increased for part of the year above the dry weather flow, with the underground source providing complementary water for the rest of the year and recharging naturally when not pumped. The river source actually yields more water than formerly, while the groundwater source yields about the same quantity but in a different pattern. Groundwater augmentation (3a and b) increases the river source throughout the year, but is still limited by rainfall replenishment of the aquifer. Only in the final stage of development, with artificial recharge, is the overall yield of the aquifer substantially increased (4a and b). Then the transfer and storage of previously unused peak river flows allows the aquifer to supply more water, either to direct supply or back to the river for its regulation at higher flows.

The joint development of the two sources, with artificial recharge from river to aquifer in some months and reverse flow from aquifer to regulated river in others, obviously raises complex technical and management problems. Even in the simplest circumstances, when groundwater is used as an independent source, its development is a degree more difficult than river development, in that the resource is hard to measure. The complexity of groundwater technology and operation of integrated systems has led many Water Authorities to rely heavily on the efforts of the central research organisations working in these fields. The Water Research Centre and the Institute of Geological Sciences, presently the main agencies for groundwater research, give an important service to those Water Authorities seeking to exploit groundwater more fully and more safely.

Control of groundwater abstraction

Before 1945 a landowner's common law rights to water in the rocks below his property were absolute. He could abstract an unlimited quantity of water for his own domestic or business use or for sale to others, and any water he did not need he could allow to run to waste. Where mining operations cut through an aquifer, the mining company was not obliged to prevent contamination or to conserve water by sealing the workings. Neither individual landowners nor statutory water undertakers were protected from loss of groundwater supplies as a result of their neighbours' exercise of common law rights.

The Advisory Committee on Water reported on measures for the protection of underground water in 1925 and noted the extreme inadequacy of the common law. 'The present position with regard to underground water is unsatisfactory; and ... it is certain that the community cannot afford indefinitely to neglect the problem ... It is the hope of the Advisory Committee that legislation on the subject of underground water will be found practicable at no distant date' (Advisory Committee on Water 1925: 2–3). Legislation came, but only after a delay of twenty years and further government investigation (Central Advisory Water Committee 1938).

Part III of the Water Act 1945, 'Conservation and protection of water resources', referred mainly to groundwater and introduced the first curbs on the common law rights of ordinary abstractors. But it was not thought necessary to interfere with these rights in all parts of the country as a general principle of water conservation. Rather the regulation was restricted to defined areas where the Minister of Health was satisfied *special* measures were needed to protect public or industrial supplies. The London Basin was one such area for special conservation of groundwater.

The Act required that in the defined conservation areas all proposals for constructing or extending wells and boreholes be submitted to the Minister for approval and licensing: only new works to be used solely for domestic purposes were exempt. For the first time direct controls were imposed on the quantities of water taken, and this laid the foundation of the abstraction licensing policy outlined in chapter 4. The mining problem was dealt with by requiring that proposals for new boring to prospect for or extract minerals be referred to the Minister who might insist on the incorporation of water conservation measures, and the Act made it a punishable offence to pollute spring or well water used for human consumption.

Progressive over-development of the more critical aquifers was certainly slowed as a result of this legislation, but there were no general, nationwide safeguards for groundwater, nor was there information enough to be sure that the measures taken in the conservation areas were sufficiently rigorous to secure future supplies here.

The Water Resources Act 1963 extended licensing control to all groundwater abstractions except the purely domestic and this, together with new investigations of groundwater supplies, gave much more comprehensive and detailed information about existing resources and the demands upon them. The Water Resources Board encouraged an intensification of research into groundwater behaviour, and its own fundamental work in this field underlies several of the current development schemes.

The licensing of abstractions has not in itself corrected all cases of over-development since, as with surface sources, licences of right permit the continuation of pre-1963 abstractions, and these alone may be in excess of the natural replenishment rate. Groundwater 'mining' is no longer an acute problem, but several major aquifers remain substantially dewatered because the volumes of licensed abstractions do not permit them to recover naturally.

Yet groundwater development has certain advantages over surface water development, prominent among them being the storage it provides with very little surface disturbance and the possibility of incremental exploitation, with one section of an aquifer developed after another as demand increases and capital becomes available. In times of extreme drought it may have additional advantages, in that an emergency water supply can be got quickly, fairly cheaply, and without permanent storage structures. In consequence groundwater might become relatively more important in the future. The management techniques currently being tested or implemented – conjunction use with surface sources, groundwater augmentation of river flows, and artificial recharge – are a response to this challenge. Groundwater abstractions for direct supply will no doubt continue and perhaps even increase, but a wider variety of techniques is coming to be used to improve efficiency in the management of both ground and surface waters.

Conjunctive use of groundwater and surface sources

Conventional groundwater development at individual sites will not disappear overnight but it is likely to give way gradually to integrated use of groundwater and surface sources, since this allows more intensive use of each. Conjunctive use is the alternating deployment of sources, groundwater being pumped when abstraction from surface sources is limited by low flows. The river flows themselves are not supplemented by groundwater, but groundwater has a balancing effect as it prevents the depletion of river flows during dry weather by giving an alternative source of supply. The first conjunctive use scheme is being developed in the Fylde area of Lancashire, where the Bunter Sandstone is to be pumped in conjunction with abstractions from the River Lune and from storage in the Stocks reservoir in the Pennines. The yield of the scheme, authorised by Ministerial Order in 1975, is expected to be in excess of 316 Ml/d, which represents a net increase of about 180 ml/d over the yield of the existing sources as at present operated (North West Water Authority 1975:21).

The scheme provides for a river intake on the Lune and a tunnel transfer of water into the adjacent Wyre basin, where the well field is sited. This and the extension of the well field will allow the Stocks reservoir to be taken out of service temporarily so that it can be enlarged for its later inclusion in the scheme. Part of the reservoir capacity might also be used for regulation of flows in the River Hodder. Indeed there is scope for integrating the Lancashire Conjunctive Use Scheme with other resources in the North West to meet water deficiencies over a wide area. The River Lune could be regulated by discharges from an enlarged Haweswater; Stocks and Rivington reservoirs used as river regulators; and the bulk supplies from the Lake District aqueducts rearranged somewhat to give a flexible, inter-linked supply system for most of the North West region (see figure 11, p. 50).

In several parts of the country the quality of groundwater makes it unsuitable for supply, and any development of aquifers must be controlled to prevent the inflow of poor quality groundwater. The Bunter Sandstone of the Fylde has two potential sources of contamination: on the west, along the coast where saline water has already been drawn into the aquifer; and at the junction with the Keuper Marl, the groundwater of which is mineralised. The development scheme for the Fylde will draw the water table down periodically below previously recorded levels, but the inflow of surrounding poor water can be prevented by maintaining positive hydraulic gradients as barriers at the boundaries. This requires carefully regulated pumping in a phased development, testing the behaviour of the aquifer under conditions of large scale intermittent abstraction. Quality preservation is essential, for once an aquifer has been contaminated it is a difficult and usually lengthy process to restore it to a good quality source.

A second aspect of water quality is also important in schemes for conjunctive use. If the sources are of different qualities, changing from one to another or mixing water from different sources may give rise to problems in water treatment. If industrial consumers need supplies of chemically uniform quality and this uniformity cannot be achieved before the water reaches users, then advance notice from the Water Authority of the proposed change of source might enable industries to carry out their own treatment.

Groundwater augmentation of river flows

The natural contribution of groundwater to river flow decreases steadily during a prolonged dry period, an unfortunate fact for river users whose supply at this time may be totally dependent on the groundwater component of river flow. The contribution of groundwater can be increased artificially by pumping from boreholes into the river, and such groundwater augmentation could become a major method of regulating river flow, alongside releases of water from surface storage. Already a large groundwater scheme is in operation to supplement flows in the River Thames and its tributaries, the Anglian Water Authority is working on a scheme to augment the Ely Ouse and the Nar with water from the Chalk, and plans are well advanced for augmenting the Severn with water from the Shropshire Sandstone.

Aquifer storage and surface storage have several parallels in their use for river regulation. Both are managed seasonally to take up and store a proportion of the annual precipitation, to reduce wasteful or dangerously high winter flows and to increase low summer flows. An aquifer in this way is left, at the end of a dry season, with its water table lower than it would have been under natural conditions. The additional storage space thus created takes up a larger than usual proportion of the winter's rainfall and so the aquifer's 'overspill' in seepage or springflow is reduced. The groundwater component of river flow is thereby altered throughout the year, made more in the summer and less in the winter.

The first field investigations into the feasibility of groundwater augmentation were begun by the Thames Conservancy in 1966. Nine boreholes were sunk in the lower Lambourn valley, Berkshire, to extract water from the Chalk. The pumped water was then transferred to the River Lambourn to flow via the Kennet into the Thames. This pilot study confirmed that the aquifer behaved much as predicted (Thames Conservancy 1972), and work began in 1974 on a second, much larger phase of development, using both Chalk and Oolite aquifers at the headwaters of the Thames.

There is a similar two-phase development in the Great Ouse basin where the pilot study was completed in 1972 (Great Ouse Groundwater Pilot Scheme 1972b), and the productive phase has just started. The Great Ouse groundwater scheme illustrates the difficulties of developing a large resource in an area where groundwater has been widely abstracted for many centuries and where the rights of existing users of both abstracted and *in situ* water cannot be ignored.

The Thames scheme pumps groundwater into the rivers when flows fall below prescribed minima, taking groundwater intermittently, perhaps for a few weeks or months, and perhaps not every year. The Great Ouse scheme differs from it, in that the aquifer will be pumped almost continuously to intercept groundwater flow and lower groundwater levels over a very large area. Figure 17 shows the area for eventual development, in three stages over a period of twenty years or so, in which it is planned to effect a fairly uniform four metre drawdown of the water table. The purpose of lowering the water table is to stop groundwater discharge through natural springs, so that the aquifer storage can be more completely controlled. Water will then be pumped out for the support of river flows, for direct abstraction and for transfer south across the watershed into Essex, at a rate equivalent to the long-term rainfall infiltration.

The effects of the groundwater scheme upon river flows will be profound. The rivers draining the Chalk outcrop will be regulated by altering their groundwater components so that dry weather flows are increased, particularly for water quality and amenity purposes. The scheme is so large, however, that all year, not just dry season support of river flows is necessary. Where the aquifer drawdown separates a river from the water table there is no natural groundwater contribution, and pumped water must be added to even out fluctuations in the flow deriving from surface runoff. As the rivers concerned all rise on Chalk, the contribution of surface runoff is in any case small except in times of peak rainfall or snowmelt.

The scheme's yield of extra water available within the Great Ouse basin and for transfer south depends partly upon the discharge required at the system's outflow at Denver, required to flush out to sea effluent from sugar beet processing at Kings Lynn. If the situation continues unaltered, the net yield of the groundwater scheme is estimated to be 250 Ml/d. If, as proposed, the Kings Lynn effluent is improved in quality and less dilution water is needed, the necessary discharge of the Ouse system could be reduced to 114 Ml/d, increasing the net yield to 330 Ml/d. If no outflow were needed,

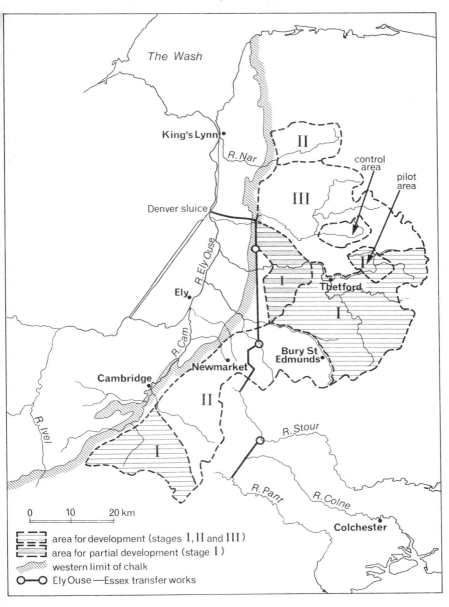

Figure 17   The Great Ouse groundwater scheme.
Based on Great Ouse River Authority 1973:24.

the net yield might rise to around 443 Ml/d. The capital costs of developing the scheme to give 330 Ml/d were estimated (at 1971 prices) to be around £18.3 m, or £23.8 m to yield 443 Ml/d (van Oosterom, Downing and Law 1973). These costs are to be compared with estimates of £25 m for 445 Ml/d from the first stage development of the Wash estuary storage scheme, and of £6.1 m for 114 Ml/d from Abbotsley reservoir, both suggested as potential sources for development after 1981 (Great Ouse River Authority 1973: 23).

Probably a net yield of 330 Ml/d is to be expected, for some outflow is needed. In the fully developed scheme the prescribed outflow at Denver is likely to have first priority, and after meeting this requirement water will be allocated for the internal demands of the Great Ouse basin, the surplus, perhaps a third or more of the net yield, being transferred south. Capital works for the transfer of Ely Ouse water to Essex were completed in 1971 and water is already diverted when flows at Denver permit it. The groundwater scheme will enable greater quantities to be taken more regularly, pumped over the watershed and discharged into the Rivers Stour and Pant (see Figure 17).

Water Resources in England and Wales considered that, apart from the Thames and Great Ouse groundwater schemes, no other source of comparable size could be developed to meet the water deficiency in south east England in the time required or 'with so little relative disruption to other interests' (Water Resources Board 1973a vol 1:41). Other interests include, in the case of the Ouse scheme, present domestic abstractors of groundwater, farmers, the Forestry Commission, the Nature Conservancy Council and fisheries associations, all of whom have reason to ask whether their activities will be adversely affected by the lowering of the water table or the alteration of flow patterns in the rivers. True as the Water Resources Board statement may be, 'little relative disruption' might still deprive a man of his livelihood or the country of a site of special scientific interest. As the scheme's Steering Committee has admitted, the groundwater scheme could have detrimental effects in three principal ways: disrupting local water supplies by drying up springs and ponds and lowering water levels in wells; reducing soil moisture to the detriment of certain crop yields; and altering the ecology of meres, marshland and rivers (Great Ouse Groundwater Pilot Study 1972b: 22).

There are several possible solutions to the problem of pre-existing water supplies. The new wells can be sited away from present sources so that the latter are affected only the general lowering of the water table and not by intense local drawdowns. The Water Authority can meet the costs of deepening or resisting private wells, if this is necessary to maintain yields. If the original water supply cannot be preserved, new connections can be made to the mains supply. In fact the Great Ouse River Authority used each of these methods in advance of pumping during the pilot study, in situations where serious disruption was predicted. Some retrospective action was also necessary where there were unexpected difficulties. Both licensed abstractions and protected (unlicensed) rights must be preserved, or alternative supplies provided, and the Water Authority hopes to meet these obligations ahead of each phase of the groundwater scheme.

Field crops and trees could be affected by lowering of the water table and loss of soil moisture, and during the pilot study the River Authority employed an agricultural adviser to investigate complaints and, where necessary, settle compensation. A liaison officer of the National Farmers' Union worked with the adviser, and this arrangement is to continue during the main development. So far, however, crop and tree damage has been slight and several sites within the pilot study area seemed to have benefited from improved drainage.

Ecological disturbance of rivers and streams, though possible and therefore investigated during the preliminary studies, also seems to be minimal. The meres and fens present a greater problem. In the development area and its vicinity there are a number of wetland sites designated as of special scientific interest, as well as many small marshy areas acting as wildlife refuges, which the Nature Conservancy Council considers could suffer significant ecological changes if the water table were lowered. There was particular concern about the regime of the Breckland meres, which resulted in a study of the feasibility of maintaining water levels by pumping water into the meres. Though it is possible to do this, a better solution appears to be the siting of abstraction wells away from the wetlands, so as to minimise artificial fluctuations in groundwater levels and to use the nearest wells only under extreme drought conditions (Great Ouse River Authority 1973: 16). As a consequence of Nature Conservancy Council and Forestry Commission interests in the Breckland west of Thetford, groundwater development here is to be restricted.

The Great Ouse groundwater scheme is not without disadvantages. The Anglian Water Authority, following the example of the Great Ouse River Authority, is attempting to minimise them through forward planning of alternative local water supplies and close liaison with special interest groups. Yet its environmental advantages heavily outweigh the disadvantages, as is clear when we compare the scheme with other means of water storage – inland reservoirs and estuary storage. The loss of land is small, mainly for wells, pumping stations and the control centre, and only the most minor changes will be observable in the landscape.

Artificial recharge of aquifers

The yield of an aquifer may be increased by artificial recharge when there is space above the existing water table and a suitable source of surface water available. *Water Resources in England and Wales* suggested that the dewatered Chalk and Tertiary Sands of the London Basin might be recharged, to become a 'strategic source' for the Thames region by the end of the century, perhaps removing the need for further surface storage in the Thames basin. It also noted the possibility of using artificial recharge as a means of improving the quality of river water, referring to experiments in filtering polluted water from the River Trent through Bunter Sandstone and River Gravels. This section considers both these aspects of artificial recharge: its contributions to quantity and to quality.

In the quantity aspect artificial recharge is the final stage of groundwater development. The earlier stages of development are – or should be – limited by the amount of natural recharge by rainfall, but artificial recharge can improve upon nature and substantially increase aquifer yield. The recharge scheme for the London Basin is to revitalise and stabilise aquifers severely over-pumped in the past and still, in some sections, with decreasing well yields.

The first suggestion of artificial recharge seems to have been that of Clutterbuck in 1850, although at that time the storage space created by over-pumping was far less than it is now. Hydrogeological conditions particularly favour recharge in the Lee valley and the Leyton–Dagenham area, where the storages in the Tertiary Sands and Chalk are estimated at around 205 million cubic metres (Lee valley) and 115 million cubic metres (Leyton–Dagenham). Since their construction towards the end of the last century the Lee valley wells have suffered substantial declines in groundwater levels and output. When the Chingford Mill station was drilled in 1884 water rose under artesian pressure 1.5 metres above the ground surface. Now water must be pumped from a depth of more than 43 metres below sea level, and the rest level of the well is 37 metres lower than it was originally. The present output is less than one quarter of the original.

The first attempts at artificial recharge in the Lee valley were before the First World War, by the East London Waterworks Company and its successor, the Metropolitan Water Board. Substantially less water was withdrawn than recharged, and the water table was raised locally by as much as 15 metres in an area where levels had been falling for many years. Then during the War the project was abandoned, and was not revived again until 1953.

In the early 1950s the rate of fall of the water table was about 0.6 m/year. At the Metropolitan Water Board's pumping station at Lee Bridge in 1953 all 16 metres of the Tertiary Sands were dewatered, together with the top 10.7 metres of the underlying Chalk. The maximum available yield of the well was less than one tenth of the original yield. The recharge experiment began at Lee Bridge in the winter of 1953–4, and river-derived filtered and chlorinated water was allowed to fall down the open well shaft. In the summer months the well was pumped as usual. By 1956 two further well stations, Ferry Lane and Chingford Mill, were included in the project, and a fourth station, Park, was added in 1962.

The last recharge season was 1968–9, and during the sixteen years of the Metropolitan Water Board's project around 25 500 Ml of water were recharged, most water going down in the earlier years. In all around 40 percent of the recharged water was recovered by abstraction, a relatively low figure probably explained by the fact that the same wells were used both for recharge and for abstraction. Water flowed with the hydraulic gradient away from the recharge wells to add to the water in storage in the aquifer and to benefit in a small degree other groundwater abstractors. The probability of escape increases with the time lag between the end of recharging and the beginning of pumping. If separate recharge and recovery wells are sited to take full benefit of the hydraulic gradients, the recovery rates may approach 100 percent (Water Resources Board 1972b: 118).

In 1969 recharge operations stopped, partly because surplus filtered water was no longer available in sufficient quantity and partly because the legal situation was unclear and the Metropolitan Water Board saw the possibility of existing groundwater users starting proceedings against it. Both these checks have now been removed. A new filtration works at Coppermills has spare capacity to prepare water for recharge, water imported from the River Thames via the Thames–Lee tunnel main. The Water Resources Act 1971 gave water agencies powers to discharge water into inland waters or underground strata, following a Ministerial Order, and new groundwater schemes for artificial recharge and river augmentation have this as their legal foundation.

The Lee valley is now entering its third period of recharge activity, with the substantial pilot scheme of the Thames Water Authority's Lee Division, following several experimental recharge cycles undertaken by the Water Resources Board. Six existing wells in the lower Lee are being modified and seven new boreholes sunk. The aquifers are widely used for public water supply and private abstraction and, as in the previous experiments, groundwater quality must be maintained. Recharge water is put directly into the aquifers, where it may move quite rapidly, and only fully treated, drinking water can be used.

One of the principal effects of the recharge project, due to start operation in 1977, will be to vary groundwater levels in the aquifers. Near the recharge and abstraction points levels will fluctuate greatly, both above and below the former range, but beyond their immediate zones of influence the fluctuations will be above former levels. In order to predict areal and temporal patterns of variation, the Water Resources Board developed a digital simulation model. To begin with a fairly crude model was used, which has since undergone progressive refinement. Initially the two aquifers were treated as one composite stratum and given combined, synthetic hydrogeological characteristics. For instance, the Tertiary Sands has an average water storage coefficient of 10 percent and the Chalk of 2 percent. The composite stratum was given a value of 5 percent. Now the model treats the

two strata separately in this respect, although it still assumes hydrauli(
continuity, that is free movement of water, between them. In some place
it seems that the Bullhead Beds (clay with flints) lying between the Sand
and Chalk may be acting as a seal and preventing this free movement. Diver
gences between observations and model predictions of groundwater beha
viour may help to pick out such anomalous areas in need of further study

Although essentially a research undertaking, the pilot scheme will be i
substantial producer of water as well as of information. The scheme i
designed to refill some 40 of the 205 million cubic metres of undergroun(
storage available in the lower Lee and to give a net increase in yield o
66 Ml/d. After the completion of the latest surface reservoir at Datche
the water supply for London is still lagging behind demand, and the yiel(
of the recharge project, going as it will entirely for London's supply, wil
be a very valuable addition to the present resource of around 1820 Ml/d. A(
advantage of the recharge project over certain alternative resource develop
ments is that the additional water can be produced quickly. In favourabl(
circumstances the full increase in yield can be achieved within two year:
of starting recharge.

The average annual cost of obtaining a yield of 66 Ml/d was calculate(
in 1973 as £368 000 or £5575 per Ml/d (Lee Conservancy Catchment Boar(
1973: 24). Operation of the project will test this calculation and give more
reliable economic data for comparison with current costs of alternativ(
resource developments. Until both economic and technical data have beer
assembled for a number of years, it is impossible to judge the potential fo(
artificial recharge as a major source of water. Only when the pilot projec(
is well advanced can decisions be taken about exploiting the rest of the
lower Lee's underground storage, giving a yield of up to 400 Ml/d. The
Water Resources Board included artificial recharge as a potential source fo(
selection towards the end of the century but noted: 'this may prove an unduly
conservative assessment; continuing investigations may establish a case fo(
its earlier development' (Water Resources Board 1973a, vol. 2: 48).

In the River Trent basin too there have been experiments in artificial
recharge. Hydrogeological conditions are quite different from those of the
London Basin, and the aquifers for recharge are the Bunter Sandstone an(
the River Gravels, both unconfined (that is in contact with the surface) an(
both acting as natural filters for water moving through them. The methods o(
recharge appropriate in the Trent basin are thus different also. To reach the
confined London Basin aquifers deep wells are necessary and since the
filtration properties of the Chalk are negligible, the water moving quickl)
along fissures in the rock, water of drinking quality only can be recharged. In
the Trent basin the aquifers can be recharged at the surface, through shallow
basins excavated for the purpose or, more simply still, by flooding or spraying water onto the undisturbed ground surface. As the water travels through
the aquifers polluting substances are removed by much the same processe:

as operate in the filtration beds of a sewage treatment works, giving an opportunity to recharge with effluent.

Experiments began in 1968 as part of the Trent Research Programme which examined the different ways in which the River Trent and its tributaries, still badly polluted by partially treated sewage and industrial effluents, could be used to meet increasing water demands. The Trent Research Programme as a whole is discussed in chapter 7; here the recharge element only is considered.

Two series of recharge experiments were carried out at Edwinstowe on the Bunter Sandstone north of Nottingham. In one series the aquifer was recharged through a basin, while in the other a nearby plot was recharged by spray irrigation, both using settled but otherwise untreated water from the River Maun. Before these experiments started the Bunter Sandstone was already used for the disposal of effluent from certain sewage treatment works, and the experimental programme included investigations of groundwater quality at two sites, Bilsthorpe and Kilton Forest Farm, where sewage effluent was spread on the surface to infiltrate the aquifer (Water Resources Board 1972c).

The cleaning effect of movement through the Bunter Sandstone was marked in the cases of basin recharge and sewage spreading, though not as striking as that noted on the spray irrigation plot. With spray irrigation hardness was greatly reduced, phosphate and anionic detergents were more efficiently removed than in basin recharge, and alkalinity and ammonia almost entirely removed. Bacteria were trapped within one metre of the ground surface. Cleaner water reached the water table, while the pollutants fertilised the vegetation and increased its yield by 225 percent compared with an unirrigated plot (Chadwick, Edworthy, Rush and Williams 1974). But the irrigation experiment was a short one: the longer-term implications are not clear. It is not yet known how long irrigation recharge could take place without damaging the soil structure, nor how long plots would take to recover from prolonged irrigation recharge and be ready for reuse. Effects upon plant associations are likewise unknown.

The River Gravels of the Trent valley are also capable of cleaning polluted water, and two methods have been investigated experimentally, one spreading polluted water onto the Gravels and allowing natural percolation to the river, and the other pumping out Gravel water to reverse the hydraulic gradient and so draw polluted river water through the aquifer for clean-up.

All these investigations were part of the now completed Trent Research Programme, with its main emphasis on pollution control. The present work on artificial recharge in the Trent basin concentrates on the supply aspect of artificial recharge, looking at possibilities for developing the Bunter Sandstone source by well recharge and then using it in conjunction with the rivers Dove and Derwent.

Table 2 lists eight possible recharge schemes for England and Wales, but

TABLE 2   *Potential artificial recharge schemes in England and Wales*

Location	Geology	Recharge by basin (B) or well (W)	Description of scheme	Estimated maximum yield Ml/day
Nottingham/ Mansfield/ Worksop area	Triassic sandstones at outcrop	B	Purification of Trent water by pretreatment and percolation	1400
Nottingham/ Mansfield area	Triassic sandstones at outcrop	W	Artificial recharge from the Derwent to augment yield of Conjunctive Use Scheme	360
London Basin	Confined Chalk and Tertiaries	W	Artificial recharge from the Thames to augment yield of combined aquifer / surface storage / river system	400
Vale of York	Triassic sandstones covered with permeable drift	W or B	Artificial recharge from the Ure and Swale to augment groundwater regulation scheme for Ouse	360
North Downs and Medway	Chalk at outcrop	W	Artificial recharge from Medway in combined river and aquifer system	270
Manchester/ Warrington/ Altrincham area	Concealed Permo-Triassic sandstones	W	Artificial recharge from Dee to augment yield of combined aquifer/surface storage/river system	230
Cilfynidd, Taff valley	Terrace gravels	B	Recharge of final sewage effluent to produce water for potable supplies	45
Hardham, Sussex	Lower Greensand	B	Artificial recharge using Rother water, in combined system	90

Based on Water Resources Board 1973a vol 2:48.

the only scheme suggested by the Water Resources Board as a 'strategic' source by the end of the century is in the London Basin where the potential is greater and investigations of its feasibility more advanced than elsewhere. This does not preclude the use of the Trent aquifers for effluent reclamation nor the development of small scale experimental-cum-productive schemes elsewhere, but it shows the hesitance of water engineers to accept artificial recharge as an immediate and major source of supply. The reasons for this are obvious. There has not been enough research on the technology and economics of recharge to convince Water Authorities that very large quantities of surface water can with safety be put underground and re-covered later at reasonable cost.

Groundwater research

Previous uncoordinated abstractions of groundwater led, as we have seen, to cases of excessive pumping, falling water levels and inflow of poor quality water from adjacent strata or the sea. It is possible now to consider the deployment of underground and surface resources together and on a regional scale, but appropriate development depends upon detailed assessments of resources and of strategies for their use. There has been much recent research in groundwater subjects – hydrological, hydrogeological, chemical, econo-mic and so on – with the central research organisations playing a very prominent part here, more prominent than in any parallel work on surface resources.

To assess a groundwater resource and determine its optimal development it is necessary, after an initial desk study has produced a possible develop-ment scheme, to test the aquifer in action by field investigations at repre-sentative sites. A pilot study, perhaps not producing water for supply, will be needed where little is known of aquifer behaviour under the particular abstraction regime. Where existing information is fuller it may be possible to proceed directly to a carefully monitored first stage of a phased develop-ment. The Great Ouse groundwater scheme is an example in the first category, the Lancashire Conjunctive Use Scheme in the second. In either case, and in addition to new abstraction wells, observation boreholes must be drilled for aquifer tests on geology and groundwater levels and quality.

Before the passage of the Water Resources Act 1963 such comprehensive studies were not feasible. Several studies of groundwater provinces had been undertaken earlier, but over most of the country development still took place in a piecemeal way from individually operated sites. Thus no overall development plans could be tested or implemented. Section 18 of the 1963 Act required River Authorities to submit proposals for groundwater investigations to the Water Resources Board for approval and, in all, the Board sanctioned thirty-three investigations and contributed to the costs of twenty-seven of them judged to yield information of benefit beyond the boundaries of the originating authority.

The Board's specialist staff were themselves actively involved in ground-water research, on their own or in collaboration with the River Authorities and statutory water undertakers. Of the Board's twenty-three publications (twenty-two series publications and a special investigation of the hydro-geology of the London Basin) six were concerned with groundwater, six with regional or national water resources, and six with estuary storage. In addition the Board published volumes on the Trent Research Programme, to which it contributed new work on artificial recharge.

The Water Resources Board's work on artificial recharge and on the development of analogue and digital models of groundwater systems is particularly important for current groundwater projects. The Water Research Association too was a major contributor in both these fields with, up to the end of 1973, five of its twenty-five groundwater publications on artificial recharge and ten on groundwater modelling.

Models of aquifer behaviour, built up from generalised data on infiltration, river flows, groundwater levels, and the aquifer's physical properties and boundaries, are calibrated and tested using historical information. Their predictive value is in the simulation of river flow and groundwater under different abstraction regimes. Hardware models using electrical resistance or resistance–capacitor analogues were built for the pilot study of the Great Ouse groundwater scheme (Great Ouse Groundwater Pilot Scheme 1971, 1972a) and for the Water Resources Board's work on artificial recharge in the London Basin (Water Resources Board 1973b), but recently digital computer models have been found more flexible, allowing new data to be incorporated more quickly. The digital model developed for the Bunter Sandstone aquifer in the Fylde, in connection with the Lancashire Conjunctive Use Scheme, indicates how such models can help in daily decisions about the operation of groups of wells.

When the 1976 drought put the better known surface sources under strain, popular attention turned for relief to imagined vast resources of water underground. *The Times*, in a front page article on 12 August, claimed that 'no good estimates exist of the water reserves available underground', and implied that a more detailed knowledge of the aquifers would yield much more water. Existing knowledge is better than *The Times* allowed, and the problems of groundwater development more subtle. There are indeed very large quantities of water in aquifer storage, but only a fraction can be withdrawn without disturbing other groundwater users and most of the surface hydrologic system as well. Current research is concerned less with the gross estimation of quantities in storage than with identifying the effects and costs of alternative ways of using the small amount of storage that is exploitable.

CHAPTER 6

FLOOD DAMAGE REDUCTION

Water is an infinitely useful commodity, but man can use it only if it behaves moderately. The appearance of water in too large a quantity or in the wrong place can cause greater hardship than its prolonged absence, and in England and Wales a sudden flood is a far more horrifying threat than is a slowly intensifying drought. In excess, water is an unwanted commodity when it breaks out of the river channel and damages the property and livelihoods of people nearby.

Most of the more serious flood events generate a demand for the Water Authorities to build flood protection works. For the Water Authorities have a responsibility, carried forward from the Land Drainage Act 1930, to protect against flooding, and the principal means of protection has been the construction of engineering works on the rivers. Flood protection works are not technically feasible in all cases, however, and in many more they are not economically justified, comparing their construction and maintenance costs with their potential benefits in terms of damage to be prevented. Flood protection works are not necessarily the only or the best solution to the flood damage problem. This chapter looks at the range of solutions now available to the Water Authorities and suggests ways in which the broadening of approach, already evident in the work of the Severn–Trent Water Authority, might be continued further.

All natural rivers flood from time to time, and damage results unless action is taken to reduce or prevent it. Only in rare and completely controlled circumstances can a river be confined permanently to a single narrow channel. Damage-reducing actions themselves carry a cost and thus, whether or not flood damage is actually averted, there is always a cost as well as a physical danger in living close to a river. The benefits of a flood-plain location may outweight this cost: clearly they often do. The practical problem is an economic one, to balance the costs and benefits of the flood-plain so that both excessive damage and excessive expenditure on damage-reducing measures are prevented, and that the advantages of the floodplain are enjoyed and exploited as long as the benefits of doing so exceed the costs.

Nixon (1963) pointed out that many of the current flood problems in England and Wales were created by ill-advised development in the nineteenth century, when rapidly increasing urban populations were housed, in ignorance of the hazard and without much thought for health, on low-lying floodplain land below the original town centres. Figure 18 shows how the earliest development at Nottingham was not on the banks of the River Trent but a little uphill. Then, from the mid 1800s, there was extensive development on both sides of the river. This newer Nottingham suffered badly from the flood of 1947; the serious floods of 1795 and 1875 caused far less disturbance as the waters then barely reached the built-up area.

While the major flood problems of today may be of comparatively recent origin, there have been floods and flood damage throughout history, and they have been treated by three traditional remedies. First, when flood hazard areas were recognised they were avoided for settlement. Many early Saxon settlements were established on the river terraces, close to the river but raised above the floodplain. Floodplain land was worked later on, but still the settlements and routeways chose the higher ground, picking out minor undulations in the valley floor. Not until the Industrial Revolution were people attracted to settle in large numbers on the floodplain.

Avoidance of the hazard had a second, more transient aspect. In times of stormy weather, prolonged heavy rains or sudden snowmelt people would watch the river and the sky and evacuate to higher ground when danger threatened. A stable population and a long collective memory were the essentials of both these avoidance strategies, with intimate local knowledge of the river's flood history being passed on from one generation to the next.

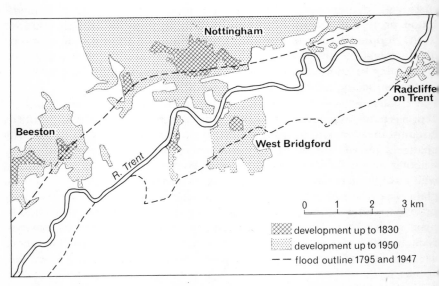

Figure 18   Development on the Trent floodplain at Nottingham
After Nixon 1963:138.

Much of this knowledge was lost or ignored in the turmoil of the nineteenth century.

The third traditional remedy against flood damage was engineering work on the river, usually in the form of flood banks or walls to contain the high flows as they passed a settlement. The Romans built flood defences for coastal and estuary sites and began the reclamation of the Thames floodplain at London. What appears to be the Roman river wall in the City is being excavated at present, and preliminary studies suggest that the wall may itself have been destroyed by flooding. But apart from the reclamation of the East Anglian Fens in the seventeenth century, most of the flood protection works were modest and of very localised efficacy.

The Court of Sewers Act 1531 was one of the earliest pieces of legislation giving local bodies powers to carry out flood protection and land drainage works, but only after 1930 and the Land Drainage Act was there the beginning of a national approach to the problem. The Land Drainage Act gave the Catchment Boards powers for flood protection on defined 'main' rivers, and since then many thousands of flood protection schemes have been constructed. In the Trent basin alone there have been well over a thousand schemes, some large, some very small, and between twenty and thirty schemes are underway there at any one time, in planning or construction stages.

Reducing flood damage in theory and practice

Flood damage results from the interaction of water and man on the floodplain, and the methods of reducing or controlling damage can tackle either the flood water or man's activities affected by it. Four main approaches can be distinguished:

1 modifying the flood,
2 modifying the damage susceptibility,
3 modifying the burden of loss, and
4 bearing the loss,

and under these headings table 3 lists the alternatives, which may be used in combination as well as singly.

The engineering methods of flood protection, controlling the water in the river channel, are well known (for example Nixon 1963; Marsland 1966; Jamieson 1972). Watershed management aims to control floods before they get to the channel, slowing runoff from the land by terracing, contour ploughing, planting of close cover crops and so on. Weather modification is sometimes suggested as another possible means of controlling floods (United States Federal Committee for Science and Technology 1971), but as yet it is not known how to alter the weather in a sufficiently reliable and consistent way.

A second approach to reducing flood damage is to modify the susceptibil-

TABLE 3   *Alternative adjustments to floods*

Modify the flood	Modify the damage susceptibility	Modify the loss burden	Bear the loss
Flood protection	*Floodplain management*	*Redistribute losses*	*Bear the loss*
Dikes	Land use regulation	Disaster relief	
Floodwalls	Urban renewal	Flood insurance	
Channel improvements	Government purchase	Reconstruction	
Floodways	of property	grants	
River diversions	Subsidised relocation	Tax write-offs	
Reservoirs			
Watershed management	*Flood proofing*		
Terracing	Use of impervious		
Gully control	construction materials		
Bank stabilisation	Land elevation		
Forest fire control	Construction on stilts		
Revegetation	Installation of		
	removable covers for		
	windows and doors		
	Closure of sewer		
	valves		
Weather modification	*Emergency measures*		
Storm seeding	Flood fighting		
	Flood warning		
	Evacuation		

ity to damage of property and activities in the floodplain. This can be achieved by regulating the type of land use in the floodplain, by making structural changes to buildings to render them permanently resistant to water, or by making changes which allow the temporary flood proofing of buildings, on receipt of a flood warning. Damage susceptibility can also be reduced by emergency evacuation of people and property, and by flood fighting.

A third approach is to modify the burden of financial loss, by spreading it over a larger section of the community than those immediately affected, as with a disaster fund, or by spreading it more evenly over time, as with flood insurance. With these adjustments the flood and its damage still occur, but the financial impact on individuals is much reduced.

The final alternative is to do nothing except bear the loss when it comes. While it may not be worth while in some places to try to *reduce* the potential damage, because the costs of achieving a reduction outweigh the benefits, bearing the financial loss unaided is an excessively negative approach when flood insurance is available.

Some of these methods can be used by individuals, irrespective of the actions of their neighbours or of the government. Flood insurance and permanent flood proofing are in this category. Other methods require corporate action for organisation, execution or finance, land use regulation, flood protection works and flood warning systems for example being impossible without some form of coordinated, group effort. And flood insurance, an individual adjustment from the point of view of the property owner purchasing it, is also a corporate enterprise, government-organised in some countries (the United States, for example) and privately-organised here.

Not only are some flood adjustments individual and others group actions, but the appropriate group or organisation varies. Adjustments to do with the river – predicting and containing high flows – are most properly the province of an organisation which looks after other aspects of water management. Adjustments to do with the land – watershed management and land use regulation – are the province of agricultural and forestry advisers and land use planners, who see flood damage reduction beside non-hydrologic considerations in land management. Emergency evacuation and rehousing of flood victims are part of the local authorities' general responsibility for dealing with disruption caused by natural disaster and civil commotion.

The Water Authorities' first involvement in flood damage reduction is with engineering works. Their flood protection works are impressive, both in numbers and in the variety of solutions they provide. River regulation reservoirs are coming to play an important part in reducing peak flows, and the Derwent in Derbyshire and the Dee in Wales both benefit from regulation storage in the headwaters. Regulation effects decrease downstream, however, as unregulated tributaries bring in high flows, and lower down a river system local flood protection works are needed. For example, Nottingham has an embankment scheme, with a widened and straightened channel and a downstream sluice to regulate the passage of water through the embanked section. The River Beam at Dagenham, Essex has been altered to give a storage area for flood flows, and Spalding in Lincolnshire is provided with a relief channel to take off the floodwaters of the River Welland.

In 1947 the water agencies, then Catchment Boards, were given an additional responsibility to cooperate with the town planners to prevent building in flood hazard areas. The Conservators of the River Thames had appreciated for some time the need to regulate indiscriminate and dangerous development on the floodplain, and in June 1936 they resolved to point this out to the town planning authorities: 'having regard to the possible danger of injury to health and the abnormal expenditure likely to be involved in the provision of land drainage works and other public services' (Conservators of the River Thames 1936). Prevention is better and cheaper than cure, was their argument.

The Ministry of Town and Country Planning asked the local planning authorities to contact the water agencies to find out about areas with drainage and flood problems, and in 1962 a second government circular re-emphasised the need for consultation (Ministry of Town and Country Planning 1947; Ministry of Housing and Local Government and Ministry of Agriculture, Fisheries and Food 1962).

Flood forecasting is the third flood adjustment falling within the province of the Water Authorities, and a relatively recent addition. For forecasting relies on long-term observations of the response of rivers to rainfall, snow-melt and water levels in the tributaries, observations only now being accumulated and analysed in sufficient numbers to give reliable predictions. *British Rainfall* and *Surface Water Yearbook of Great Britain* were already collecting and publishing rainfall and river flow records, but the number of observation points was small until comprehensive hydrometric schemes were encouraged by the Water Resources Act 1963.

A flood forecast, albeit timely and accurate, is of academic interest only unless it is transformed into a public warning of danger so that damage-reducing measures can be put into effect. The Water Authorities' task is limited to flood forecasting and the notification of the police that river overflow is expected. It is the responsibility of the police to issue public warnings and to alert other services that may be needed during the emergency. Rapid and unambiguous communication between the Water Authorities and the police is essential for the effective organisation of emergency measures.

The other possible adjustments to the flood hazard listed in table 3 are outside the control of the Water Authorities. It is up to the individual to decide whether or not to flood proof his building, or to insure it against flood damage. The insurance companies are free to fix premiums to reflect the degree of risk as they see it, a perception that may differ markedly from that of the Water Authority. Without implying that these individual freedoms be constrained, one can suggest that closer connections with the Water Authorities would improve the individual choices.

There are two separate arguments here. One is that more precise information about the nature and degree of hazard would assist rational choice, for example by enabling the property owner to select the most appropriate type of structural alterations to his building, or by showing the insurance companies the areal patterns of flood risk. In practice the public gets almost no help from the Water Authorities unless it seeks it in a most deliberate and persevering manner, but many people who would benefit from more information at present know so little about the flood hazard that they do not see their predicament.

The second argument for closer connection between the Water Authorities' set of damage-reducing measures and all other such measures is a financial one. When a Water Authority builds flood protection works, the protected community pays no more than all other communities in the area (the local land drainage district), some of which may be in dangerous positions but without protection. There is no specific charge on the protected community. If a community seeks flood protection but is refused it on the grounds that a scheme would be too costly in relation to the expected benefits, the owners of vulnerable properties are left with the choice of doing nothing and facing damage when it comes, buying flood insurance, perhaps at very high premiums, or having the properties flood proofed. All three alternatives place the entire costs on the individuals who, in only slightly different circumstances, would have been given protection free of charge. The present dilemma is that if an engineering scheme is not justified, no financial help can be given to enable people to adopt other damage-reducing measures. Probably all the vulnerable community will do in these circumstances is wait for another flood and renew its demand for protection.

Engineering works for flood protection

The River Trent basin, the subject of this study, is well provided with flood protection works. The Ladybower reservoir helps to control peak flows on the Derwent, there are earthen flood banks along the lower, tidal section of the Trent, two elaborate schemes for the protection of Nottingham from the Trent and its tributary the Leen, and a multitude of smaller works upstream of Nottingham. Over a thousand schemes have been completed in the last forty years, yet there is still no reduction in the demand for flood protection.

There is, however, a noticeable change in the purpose of the schemes. Formerly they were designed for areas which had suffered flooding in the past, the demand for protection coming on the heels of a flood event.* The majority of the larger settlements previously flooded have now been successful in their demands. The present and future need is for engineering work to cope with the increased runoff from new development. When permeable rural areas are covered with buildings, roads and pavements and are sewered into the river, the rate of runoff is greatly increased. Downstream flood conditions will be exacerbated unless flood storage can be provided upstream or the watercourse improved in anticipation of increased flood peaks. Proposals for land drainage and flood protection in the River Idle took account of increased flows due to future urban development throughout the catchment and in particular in the Mansfield–Alfreton growth area (Severn–Trent Water Authority 1974a).

The term 'flood protection' is perhaps a misleading one, since complete protection can never be given. There is always the possibility that a flood larger than the design flood will come to overtop the scheme and inundate the protected area: protection is partial and a residual hazard remains. The desired level of protection – the design flood – has to be selected from the range of possibilities. One very straightforward approach, widely used all over the country, is to choose a level of protection a little greater than the flood that generated the demand for the scheme. While crude and indeed no proper selection, since alternatives are not considered, this is not without

* Referring to the country as a whole, Johnson (1973) suggested that about three quarters of the expensive schemes have been undertaken as a consequence of a flood occurring.

merit. Protection against a flood like the 1968 flood, say, is something easily understood by the public, to whom it seems to have a rational basis. It is also less difficult to assess the scheme's worthwhileness when information has been assembled about actual flood damage in the recent past. But the limitations are obvious. Roberts (1973) suggested that this method had left some communities with protection against floods with return periods of up to thirty years and others with protection against rare and catastrophic events. The most appropriate level of protection, considering human safety, damage to be prevented in the long term and associated costs, may be either higher or lower than what might be termed the 'demand flood'.

Rather than equate design flood with demand flood, the Severn–Trent Water Authority now designs to protect against floods up to the once in a hundred year event. While the level of protection is stated with precision, along with the residual hazard, it is less clear why of all possible flood frequencies the hundred-year flood should have been chosen. It may still not be the result of a rational selection. A full consideration of alternatives must wait until the Water Authorities have the manpower and facilities to compute costs and benefits of different levels of protection given by several alternative schemes. At present it is difficult enough to assemble data for a single scheme.

The Water Act 1973 brought an immediate change in the financing of many water services but not of land drainage and flood protection. These continue to be financed by precepts on local authorities and internal drainage boards, by general drainage charges on landowners and by government grants. The Water Act provided that funds raised by precept in any one district should be used for the benefit of that district, and the local Land Drainage Committees – new statutory creations of the Act – determine the necessary programme of work and thus the level of local precept. Capital programmes are submitted for approval to the Regional Land Drainage Committee of the Water Authority, and then to the Ministry of Agriculture, Fisheries and Food for approval and grant-aid.

Schemes for grant-aid must be submitted with full technical details, estimated costs and estimated potential benefits. The Severn–Trent Water Authority also undertakes its own cost–benefit analyses of all new schemes for the Trent basin, whether grant-aided or not, an exercise considered necessary as the more urgently needed and obviously beneficial schemes have already been completed.

A central, practical problem in cost–benefit studies of flood protection works is the identification of benefits. Benefits are the reductions in damage, both tangible and intangible, brought about by the scheme but, since even the most obvious types of damage have not been recorded systematically in the past, the necessary figures are difficult to supply. A memorandum from the Ministry of Agriculture, Fisheries and Food (1974) advised Water Authorities on the preparation of reports on land drainage and flood protection required under section 24(5) of the Water Act 1973. It detailed the type of information to be assembled about the physical hazard, the property at risk and the potential damage to be expected from floods of various magnitudes and frequencies, necessary for the calculation of cost–benefit ratios and the ordering of priorities. Roberts (1973) had pointed to the need for such guidelines from central government, and suggested that approved programmes to collect the necessary data should themselves be grant-aided. Certainly such data collection is a vital but very demanding task, and later we look at some recent endeavours to make it less onerous and the results more reliable.

Land use regulation to control flood damage

In addition to keeping floods away from the people, one can regulate the types of land use in the floodplain to keep people away from the floods. Regulation of the floodplain has two main applications. In areas not protected by engineering works, regulation can maintain a pattern of land use which is not severely affected by flooding, preserving a comparatively low damage potential by directing more vulnerable land uses elsewhere. In areas where protection works *have* been built, there is a danger that the residual hazard may be underestimated and dangerously inappropriate land uses developed in the protected area. Land use regulation can help developers take advantage of the real improvement in safety, without over-shooting into the realms of imagination.

Nor is the relevance of land use regulation for controlling flood damage confined to the floodplain. If extensive urban development takes place in a small river basin, floods may increase in frequency and magnitude, affecting downstream areas previously flood-free. If the Water Authorities are not to be forced into further constructional activity to protect downstream communities, the new urban developments must themselves incorporate flood control measures to slow the rate of delivery of water to the river.

The government circulars which are the basis of cooperation between local planning authorities and Water Authorities acknowledge both the floodplain and the wider, catchment area aspects of the flood damage problem. That of 1962 asked the water agencies to inform planners 'of the areas where development is likely to give rise to drainage problems and in particular of the extent of the floodplains and/or washlands of their rivers' and most have by now responded with maps of flood hazard areas. Planning authorities were asked to consult before granting permission for development within the areas so indicated, and a circular in 1969 stressed again the need for consultation over surface runoff from proposed new developments (Ministry of Housing and Local Government and Welsh Office 1969).

The direct powers of a Water Authority stop short at the top of the river banks, and beyond this point it must rely on the planning authority to safeguard its interests in the floodplain and catchment. That in some parts of the country the safeguards are inadequate is only too clear. Hollis (1974) cited the case of development on the Thames and Mole floodplains at Molesey, Surrey, where intense pressure for housing outweighed the pleas of water agency (the Thames Conservancy) and county planners alike for refusal of planning permission. After a public inquiry and Ministerial decision, building began in the early 1960s and the new houses were swamped by disastrous floods in September 1968. Floodplain encroachment continues today, in areas where the liaison advocated in the circulars is weak or where pressure on land is exceptionally strong, and Penning-Rowsell and Parker (1974) have suggested that statutory controls may be needed, with special development control procedures being applied in areas designated as liable to flooding.

Before the reorganisation of local government and of the water industry in 1974, the Trent River Authority had contacts with eighteen planning authorities. Now the Severn–Trent Water Authority deals with around sixty separate planning units in the Trent basin. The precise form of contact was first discussed with the chief officers of all the planning authorities in 1965, and the same year the planners were issued with floodplain maps of 'main' rivers. After the local government reorganisation the basis for consultation was redefined for the benefit of the new planning authorities.

For the purpose of land use regulation, the floodplains of the Trent and its tributaries are divided into three zones, according to their damage characteristics and their hydraulic importance to the river regime:

Zone 1   That area of the floodplain which is required to pass the flood discharge of the river at the normal gradient and velocity. This is sometimes termed 'floodway'.

Zone 2   That area of the floodplain whose main function is to store water until falling levels downstream allow it to flow away. This is termed 'washland'.

Zone 3   That area of the floodplain which comes into use only during rare or catastrophic floods.

(Sterland and Nixon 1972: 34–5)

Any development in zone 1, the floodway, would risk severe damage from flowing water and might constrict the floodway so that the discharge capacity was reduced and floodwater built up behind the obstruction. Here the Water Authority recommends complete prohibition of development, except in essential cases where, for instance, a motorway route crosses the valley. Then the openings in the motorway support must be adequate to pass the flood discharge without raising water levels upstream.

In zone 2, the washland, development is restricted to that which does not decrease flood storage capacity. There are no objections to open uses such as recreation grounds, boatyards, car parks and so on, nor to certain more obstructive developments, as long as compensatory storage is provided. Ground levels may be remoulded so that a flat, raised section is available for building use, with an adjacent section deepened in compensation.

In zone 3 which floods only rarely the Water Authority recommends no restriction on development, but suggests precautionary measures such as raising floor levels or electrical installations above the highest known flood level.

Since flood magnitude is variable, the washland area of a small and frequent flood will be the main floodway of a larger and rare event. There can be no absolute division of the floodplain into zones, as different parts fulfill different functions according to the magnitude of the flood. In the Trent valley the zones are separated, using the 25-year flood as the base. Zones 1 and 2 are not differentiated on the floodplain maps and are separated only in detailed local studies. The outer boundary of zone 2 is the outline of the 25-year flood, determined sometimes from recorded flood outlines, sometimes by calculation and occasionally by aerial photography. Figure 19 is part of a floodplain map for the River Tame. The outer boundary of zone 3 is plotted on open land 4 feet (1.2 metres) above the 25-year flood line and in narrow valleys at a higher level.

The Water Authority's approach to the regulation of land use on the Trent floodplain is a sophisticated one, defining different hydraulic functions and different damage potentials across the floodplain and recommending variable controls to suit these conditions, but it is for the planning authority to decide whether or not to accept these recommendations. Over the last decade the water agency for the Trent has received between 1500 and 2000 referrals a year from the planners concerning proposed developments which might affect or be affected by flooding. When the water agency has objected to a development the planners have almost invariably refused development permission. If the developer has then appealed against the decision, the refusal has been upheld.

Nonetheless land use planning on the floodplain could be further improved at the fringe of the hazard area, where development is not prohibited but where the Water Authority recommends flood proofing measures. Sometimes planners incorporate a flood proofing recommendation as a condition in the building permit, but often advice is not passed on to the developer. The Water Authority does not itself undertake flood proofing work but might give technical help on both methods and design standards, if developers and the Water Authority were in closer contact. At present useful information is being lost in transmission via the local authority planners.

Flood proofing measures

Flood proofing is the design or alteration of individual buildings with the primary aim of reducing flood damage, and flood proofing measures can be separated into three categories, depending on their permanence. *Permanent* flood proofing does not require any judgement, flood warning or action to

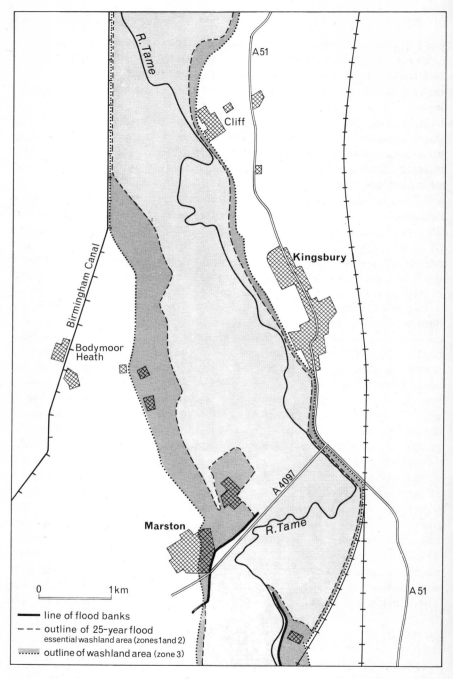

Figure 19   Part of a floodplain map for the River Tame, Severn–Trent Water Authority.

put the measures into effect. A building is designed originally or altered later so that no further damage-reducing action is needed. Houses or office blocks built on stilts are examples. *Contingent* flood proofing is not effective unless, on receipt of the flood warning, some minimum action is taken to make the measures operational. An example is the protection of windows and doors by hinged or sliding metal shields. The shields are in place beside the openings, to be moved to seal them off only in an emergency (figure 20). *Emergency* or *temporary* flood proofing measures are either improvised just before or during a flood or are carried out according to an established emergency plan. Boarding and sand-bagging of openings are in this category.

The recommendations of the Severn–Trent Water Authority concerning buildings in zone 3 of the floodplain are normally for permanent flood proofing measures. The raising of ground floor levels, on fill or stilts, the raising of electrical installations, the provision of refuge rooms above flood level and the provision of escape routes through bungalow roofs have all been suggested and in some cases put into effect.

Emergency flood proofing is widely practised, for anyone will try to prevent water entering his house if he has the opportunity to do so. In the past the improvisation element has been large and the planned element almost non-existent, but recent improvements in flood forecasting and warning have led to more concern for emergency planning and coordination.

It is perhaps in the field of contingent flood proofing that the greatest advance could be made, especially for commercial and industrial premises whose flood losses may be very large. These measures, extremely efficient in water proofing, are useful on existing buildings where the flood hazard was recognised too late for permanent measures. Contingent flood proofing of a group of buildings may well be cheaper than engineering works on the river. The reluctance to adopt such measures comes partly from the property owners' ignorance of the hazard and partly from the high private costs.

Flood warning and emergency action

Emergency action on receipt of a reliable flood warning can do much to reduce flood damage, by maintaining flood defences against breaching or overtopping, temporarily flood proofing buildings and raising contents and, as the danger intensifies, evacuating people and their movable belongings. The efficacy of emergency action depends on the accuracy of the flood forecast, on the length of warning time given, and on the organisational preparedness in the hazard area (Day 1973). The last is by far the most complex aspect, since many different organisations are involved, between whom specific flood responsibilities are divided.

We have already noted the separation of flood forecasting and flood warning, the Water Authorities being responsible for the one, the police for the other. The Trent River Board was concerned with flood forecasting from its

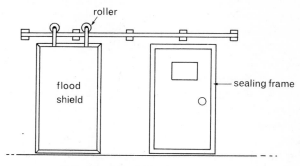

sliding flood shield for door

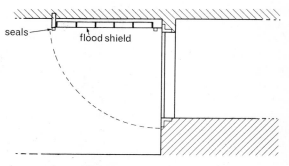

hinged flood shield for loading dock

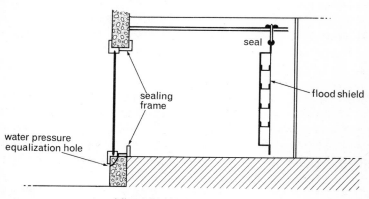

stored flood shield behind window

Figure 20   Flood shield installations for flood proofing.
Source: United States Army, Office of the Chief of Engineers 1972:14–16.

inception in 1948, but systematic instrumentation in the catchment during the last decade has given a markedly improved forecasting service recently. Improvements in instrumentation continue, and a new scheme based on telemetry is being implemented currently, due for completion in 1978.

Flash floods due to intense thunderstorms in small catchments may escape the most vigilant instrument net, and in any case may rise so fast that no advance notice can be given. The flood forecasting service for the Trent basin concentrates instead on the prediction of flooding on the larger rivers and affecting the main centres of urban population. In Derby and Nottingham for example twenty-four or thirty-six hours notice may be possible, allowing very considerable readjustment in the hazard areas.

Basic information for the forecasting service comes from the Meteorological Office, and from the Authority's own rainfall and river gauges. When peak flows on the headwater streams are known or are predicted from present and antecedent precipitation, the peaks are traced down through the river system by correlation of river levels. Overspill from reservoirs is taken into account, as is the tidal situation on the lower Trent.

The accuracy of the forecast depends both on the correlation model and on the number and accuracy of the observations supplied to it. At present the Trent basin has seventeen rain gauges and twenty river level recorders which are regularly interrogated by telephone every weekday morning, and more frequently when flooding is likely. In addition there are now five direct alarms which will dial out with pre-recorded messages of critical conditions. A computerised system for scanning observation stations and predicting river levels is a third phase of development of the forecasting service, and when this is completed, fifty stations will be scanned automatically every fifteen minutes. No major increase in the length of warning time is expected from the new system, but it should produce more accurate forecasts of maximum levels, essential information for determining areas of probable overflow and assessing the likely fate of flood protection works.

Figure 21 outlines the present forecasting service, operated by the Water Resources Section, and shows the forecast passed on to the police and to the Authority's own flood fighting forces in the 'areas' of the river basin. Each area has its own flood emergency procedure suitable to local conditions. Work gangs with vehicles, sand bags and other equipment can be mustered at short notice, and the Water Authority has a stand-by arrangement to call in additional help from the Army, should the emergency demand it.

All other aspects of emergency action are outside the control of the Water Authority. Formerly the Civil Defence organisation arranged evacuation, temporary housing and emergency supplies of food and clothing for flood victims, and helped too in less extreme situations with raising or moving household goods. The disbanding of the Civil Defence left an organisational gap, filled in the case of Nottingham by an emergency coordinator on the staff of the local authority. Clearly many organisations may be involved:

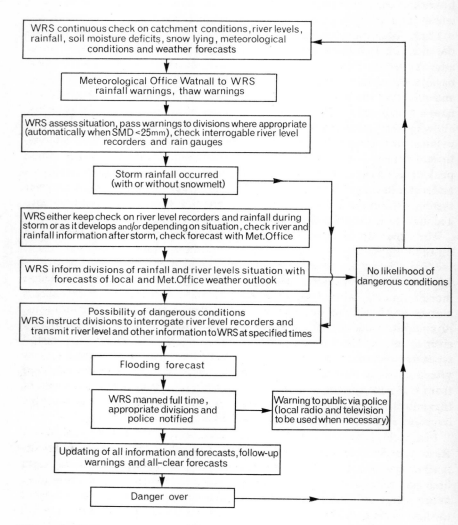

WRS   Water Resources Section
SMD   soil moisture deficit

Figure 21   Flood forecasting system for the Trent valley.
Source: Trent River Authority 1970.

the police and the Automobile Association in closing roads and redirecting traffic; voluntary organisations such as the Red Cross and the WRVS in providing meals and dry clothes; and many branches of the local authorities' social services, giving assistance both during and after the flood event. The need for coordination is self-evident. Harding and Parker (1974) have described in detail the emergency plan for Shrewsbury, on the River Severn, summarised in figure 22. It is essential that responsibilities be defined precisely and the degrees of flood warning and appropriate time for the various emergency actions properly understood, so that each organisation can work independently, should normal communications be disrupted.

As the staff of these organisations change and the memory of the last flood emergency fades, so the familiarity with the emergency plan fades. Regular training conferences are necessary to keep the plan and its potential implementors up to date. One such conference took place recently, to define the roles of Nottingham's emergency coordinator, the police, the Army and the Severn–Trent Water Authority in relation to flooding on the middle Trent.

Flood insurance

The adjustments considered so far seek to reduce flood damage or to prevent increases in damage potential. Flood insurance is different, in that damage is accepted. The purpose of insurance is to accumulate small, regular premiums against the possibility of large, irregularly occurring losses. Time-averaging is rather more important in flood insurance than in most other types of insurance, partly because of the highly variable loss from year to year and partly because the flood hazard is restricted in its distribution and there is a tendency for only those people who recognise their exposure to it to seek insurance. The areal spread of risk obtained by insurers depends largely on the way flood insurance is offered to the public.

Insurance against flooding began after the First World War, although as early as 1874 there were proposals for such insurance, following on practice in France and Italy. In France communes were rated by the number of times flooded, with statistics on flood events dating from 1826, and within communes there was some variation of rate with elevation. Cornelius Walford (1876: 187) lamented that in Britain 'We have, with all our elaborate machinery of Gov. no department in which useful statistics, such as those readily obtained in France, are compiled. . . The necessary facts, then, on which to base operations, can only be obtained by private enterprise. We have commenced the compilation of a register of localities periodically subjected to floods.' Insurance is still characterised by individual enterprise, both in data collection and in underwriting.

Flood insurance met its greatest challenge in 1960 and 1961, when the

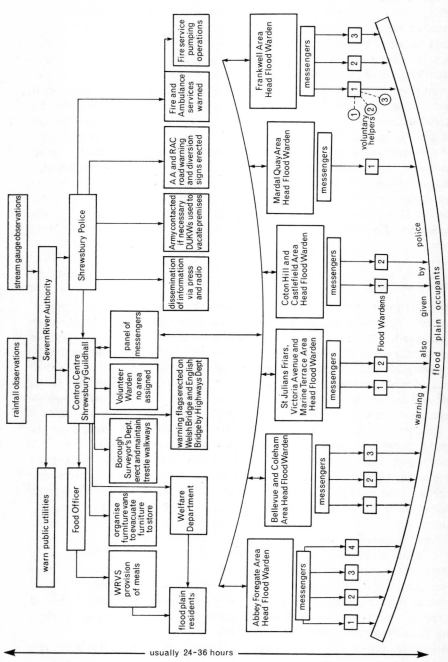

Figure 22 Flood warning and emergency plan for Shrewsbury.

central government considered a public demand for a national disaster fund. The autumn and winter floods of 1960 generated a flow of letters to government departments about a disaster fund, and the Minister of Housing and Local Government contacted the British Insurance Association because many of the requests mentioned or implied absence of flood insurance. Insurers claimed that in all but a very few cases 'the blame for the absence of insurance cover could be laid fairly and squarely at the door of the victims themselves for neglecting to insure their household goods' (The Policyholder 1961) but even so they thought it prudent to publicise an offer of increased flood cover. Since 1961 insurers have never refused to insure the contents of houses against floods, however high the risk, although premiums may be much higher than the standard rate. As a result of the insurance industry's action, and considering local government powers and local appeal funds, the government decided that a national disaster fund was unnecessary.

Insurers desire premiums for flood insurance to be directly related to financial risk, the annual premium covering the annual long-term loss together with administrative costs and profit, but annual long-term loss is not easily determined. Walford pointed to a disabling lack of information in the last century, a situation only partially remedied now. Different degrees of risk are admitted in a most elementary way. One scheme for houses and shops has three risk classifications: 'normal' or no risk, well away from any river; property flooded on exceptional occasions; and property in notoriously bad flood areas, frequently flooded. 'Notorious' property incurs a premium twenty times higher than 'normal' property. In 1964 a group of insurers felt a need to improve risk assessment techniques and asked the Hydraulics Research Station, Wallingford, for advice. The reply dealt with the concept of flood frequency. It set out a statistical method of computation and indicated how maps might be drawn of areas with various frequencies of flooding, but the insurers themselves have been unable to put such suggestions into practice. Rather they have from time to time sought maps of flooded areas or information about individual sites from the water agencies. The recently published *Flood Studies Report* (Natural Environment Research Council 1975), giving a national picture of flood magnitude and frequency, should advance their practical knowledge much further.

Flood damage information

Improved information on flood hazard areas, their degrees of risk in terms of frequency of flooding and the likely damage to property within them, is needed not only for the efficient operation of flood insurance but for all flood adjustments. Individual adjustments would function better, and a more rational choice between alternatives could be made, provided always that institutional arrangements allowed such a comparison. The *Flood Studies Report* has already met part of the problem, but two fundamental difficulties remain: the dearth of reliable information on flood damage; and the nature of the decision process about flood adjustments.

The Ministry of Agriculture's 'worthwhileness' or cost–benefit tests on proposed flood protection schemes have obliged water agencies to assemble what data they can on past and potential effects of flooding, and several have carried out damage surveys to justify their schemes (for example, Trent River Board 1962, 1963; Severn–Trent Water Authority 1974a). But as yet the Water Authorities' damage information has not been applied to the analysis of other flood adjustments, by the Water Authorities or by other organisations, partly because of data inadequacies.

The Institution of Civil Engineers's report *Floods in the United Kingdom* (1967) recommended that information on the damage resulting from floods be systematically collected and stored. Information assembled in the immediate post-flood period can give a fairly precise record of actual damage, although there are tendencies to underestimate some types of damage which show themselves only gradually, such as damage to woodwork, and to exaggerate others, such as loss of goods which have a salvage value. If a damage survey is delayed for many months in order to circumvent these difficulties, another set may arise in that details of damage will not be recalled clearly.

For the purposes of justifying flood protection schemes in areas where floods have occurred in the recent past, records of actual damage have an obvious value, but increasingly protection schemes and other flood adjustments are being designed in anticipation of flooding. Some method is needed to estimate potential damage in the absence of data on past flooding. Harding and Porter (1970) and Porter (1971) suggested that generalised flood damage data be developed, based on detailed surveys of selected sites but widely applicable to other sites with comparable characteristics of hydrology and land use. Part of the research effort of the Middlesex Polytechnic's 'flood hazard research project' continued further this search for generality, and data on potential damage have been produced not from surveys of past experience but from synthetic estimates of what *would* be the damage *if* a flood occurred (Parker and Chatterton 1974; Penning-Rowsell and Chatterton 1977).

Damage to defined standard floodplain land uses is plotted against depth of flood water, to give depth-damage curves, as in figure 23. Such information is applicable to groups of similar properties or land uses, knowing the level at which damage begins at each, to produce aggregate figures for expected damage under various depths and frequencies of flooding. Future changes in land use can be taken into account, as can predicted reductions or increases in the physical hazard. A basic assumption in this work is that no emergency action is taken to reduce damage: the resulting depth-damage data represent conditions of maximum loss. Where a flood warning system and emergency plan are likely to reduce damage significantly, additional

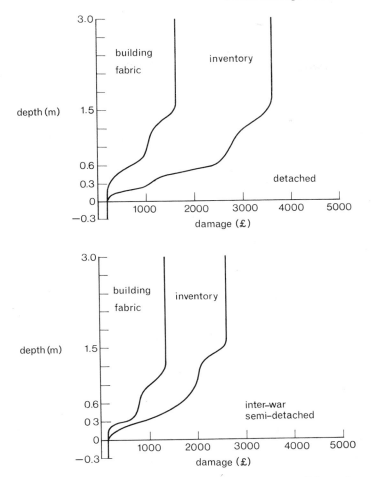

Figure 23   Depth-damage curves for residential property: conditions of maximum loss.
Source: Penning-Rowsell and Chatterton 1977:10–11.

curves, incorporating the effects of the emergency action, can be compared with the originals to measure the benefit of emergency action (figure 24). The flexibility of synthetic damage data is so much greater than that of records of actual damage that a relatively restricted effort in data collection can give worthwhile results.

Technical advances in flood frequency studies and in the development of synthetic data on flood damage make possible a comparison of the economic merits of alternative flood adjustments, but how far they will be used in practice depends as much on organisation as on technique. An institutional structure ideal for managing flood damage would allow the comparison of all

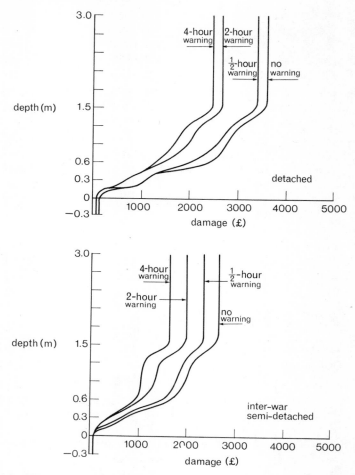

Figure 24   Depth-damage curves for residential property, showing the potential effects of flood warnings.
Source: Penning-Rowsell and Chatterton 1977:10–11.

alternative flood adjustments listed in table 3 (p. 96), according to their costs and benefits.

Floods are extremes of river flow: flood damage reduction is thus an aspect of water management. Floodplains and their susceptibility to damage are part of a larger land use system: flood damage reduction is thus an aspect of local and regional development policy. Only a structure which accommodates both these spheres of interest will be adequate. But of course water management is not an end in itself, and should in any case be viewed alongside development policies. The literal overlapping of land and water interests in the matter of flood damage reduction is no more than a particularly clear manifestation of a general difficulty. The Land Drainage Committees, established under the Water Act 1973, bringing together Water Authority and local authority interests, are an attempt to solve this problem.

Other improvements in efficiency could be achieved through a better flow of information. The Water Authorities hold basic data on flood flows and areas inundated in the past, and some, including the Severn–Trent, have delimited areas subject to different frequencies of flooding. The new magnitude–frequency material of the *Flood Studies Report* should enable all Water Authorities to reach at least this level of sophistication in defining zones of hazard. Then the question of publicity arises. If the groups and individuals who face flood problems are to act sensibly to resolve them, it is necessary that information on the hazard be distributed outside the Water Authorities. At present some Authorities are deliberately secretive, perhaps to avoid public alarm, but this certainly makes it difficult for floodplain dwellers to appreciate the nature of the risk they face. A technical report on the local flood risk would probably advance their understanding no further. A short, simple exposition is needed, maybe in the form of a pamphlet.

A second aspect of information flow is the publicising of adjustments other than engineering works for flood protection. This was seen to be so important in the Tennessee Valley Authority area of the United States that in the 1950s a 'local flood relations office' was given the task of helping the flood-prone communities for whom protection works were not feasible to find alternative means of controlling damage (Goddard 1961). Land use regulations and flood proofing techniques have been employed at hundreds of sites in the Tennessee Valley as a result. The Water Authorities here might consider a similar policy, which would not increase the Authorities' responsibility for other adjustments but would in effect pass on flood problems for which protection works were not the answer.

Finally one must ask whether the alternatives will ever seem as desirable to local people as protection works, the costs of which fall very lightly on the individuals protected. Flood insurance, flood proofing and emergency action require individual initiative, funding or physical effort, and restrictions on land use deny a land owner the financial benefits of development which would have taken place in the absence of the flood hazard. It seems inevitable that there will be continued and sustained local pressure for engineering solutions in preference to others, and the Water Authorities and the Ministry of Agriculture need not only to check that each protection scheme is worth while, with expected benefits in excess of costs, but to satisfy themselves that no other, non-engineering alternative is better. If an alternative is preferred on general economic grounds but is too expensive for the floodplain dwellers to adopt unaided, some diversion of public funds might not be out of place.

CHAPTER 7

EFFLUENT DISPOSAL AND THE CONTROL OF RIVER POLLUTION

In an urban–industrial society one of the principal demands on a water resource system is for the disposal of effluents. Within limits a river is able to acommodate liquid wastes and render them harmless – but only within limits. When the volume and strength of the incoming effluent exceed the river's capacity, there is rapid deterioration of water quality. A river channel can, of course, be used primarily as a sewer, if effluent disposal takes precedence over all other demands, and there is no shortage of examples of British rivers that have been developed in this way. They are now unsafe for water supply, devoid of fish, ugly and smelly, their multi-use possibilities very severely restricted. Yet the majority of rivers have not been given over entirely to effluent disposal. All except those in the most undeveloped rural areas do receive considerable polluting loads, but most manage to retain a range of functions. The Water Authorities are responsible for preserving and diversifying this range, to provide for effluent disposal without denying other demands on the river system.

Modest polluting loads of domestic sewage and industrial wastes usually do little harm to the river water and the life it supports because processes of self-purification soon clean up the pollutants. Substances that are harmful in high concentrations are dispersed and diluted in the river and ultimately conveyed to the sea for further dilution. Certain active chemicals are oxidised in the river and thereby rendered inactive. Complex organic substances, such as those contained in sewage, are decomposed by microorganisms into simpler substances which are then taken up by aquatic plants and recycled. As long as the receiving water is itself clean and free running, the adverse effects of a modest polluting discharge can be expected to have disappeared altogether a few miles downstream.

Over much of the country the Industrial Revolution brought two changes that upset the natural balances of self-purification. Polluting discharges increased in number and strength many times over; and as polluted reaches extended farther and farther downstream of discharge points and gradually coalesced, the quality of the receiving environment for new discharges deteriorated. The Rivers Pollution Prevention Act 1876 recognised and attempted to prohibit four types of pollution: by solid material, and by sewage, manufacturing and mine water discharges. Though controlled, these sources of pollution are with us today, together with surface water runoff, contaminated by road and pavement washings in urban areas and by farm chemicals in rural areas.

The diverse effects of these pollutants can be grouped as chemical, physical, biological or bacteriological. A common chemical effect arising from sewage discharges is a reduction in dissolved oxygen. Physical effects include increases in temperature, turbidity and rate of settlement of solid material. Fish mortality is clearly a biological effect, and the proliferation of coliform bacteria a bacteriological one. Within such a simple grouping there are important interactions. For instance, it may be that fish die through a lack of dissolved oxygen or that their spawning grounds are destroyed by deposited material.

Not surprisingly, no single measure of water quality has proved adequate for defining pollution. Before accurate analytical tests, the criteria of river 'wholesomeness' used by courts of law in disputed cases were whether cattle could drink the water and fish survive in it. Since the 1912 report of the Royal Commission on Sewage Disposal, measures of dissolved oxygen and suspended solids have been most widely applied, complemented in the cases of many industrial discharges by measures of ammonia, cyanides, phenols and so on, relevant to the particular effluent.

Probably the most trustworthy chemical index of river quality is some measure of dissolved oxygen. The Commissioners were of this opinion, and it merits brief explanation. Organic matter in sewage and many industrial discharges undergoes bacterial decomposition, and in the course of their work the aerobic bacteria consume oxygen dissolved in the river water. Large organic discharges can thereby cause severe deoxygenation, this in turn causing the cessation of decomposition and the replacement of aerobic by anaerobic bacteria which give off hydrogen sulphide – the characteristic 'bad eggs' smell of polluted or stagnant water. The rate of absorption of dissolved oxygen, measured over a period of five days, was recommended by the Commissioners as the principal test of river quality, and the five-day biochemical oxygen demand (or BOD) is still very widely used today. The higher the BOD of an effluent or stretch of river, the greater the pollution.

On the assumption that the effluent would receive at least eight times dilution with clean river water, the Commission's 1912 report recommended that, as a normal standard, sewage effluents should not take up more than 20 parts per million of dissolved oxygen (over five days at 65°F) nor contain more than 30 parts per million of suspended solids. This, the 20/30 Royal Commission standard as it is commonly known, is applied to the majority of discharges from present-day sewage treatment works.

In addition to a liquid effluent, sewage treatment works produce sludge, the solids accumulated during treatment. The greater the purification of sewage achieved, the more sludge is produced, and disposing of the sludge, by dumping at sea or applying to agricultural land, is 'the greatest problem at treatment works today', according to the Working Party on Sewage Disposal (Department of the Environment and Welsh Office 1970: 10). Toxic metals and large, stable organochlorine compounds may pass unaltered through a treatment works and be concentrated in the sludge, to become a potential hazard to organisms in the disposal areas.

Pollution prevention

The history of pollution control has been traced briefly in chapter 2. One can distinguish three phases of control, each with its own legal devices. During the long life of the Rivers Pollution Prevention Act 1876 there was simple prohibition. As the law of the ancient Persians had forbidden the discharge of organic refuse into the rivers (Klein 1967: 1), so our 1876 Act forbade any polluting discharge, and it failed because urban and industrial life could not continue under such a stricture. The essential qualification, that no offence was committed if the discharger adopted the best practical and available means of treatment, was in effect an escape clause which destroyed the Act's authority and intended purpose. Another fault of the early legislation was that it dealt exclusively with pollution from works already established. No action could be taken until an offence actually occurred, even though it might be clear that a plant or process about to set up was bound to cause pollution.

When the Rivers (Prevention of Pollution) Act 1951 replaced the 1876 Act, prohibition was abandoned and two new legal devices tried, one of which was unsuccessful and repealed ten years later. Between 1951 and 1961 the River Boards were empowered to fix by byelaw minimum standards for a whole river or river reach, with which all effluents must comply. The byelaw standards were subject to confirmation by the Minister of Health, as a check that the new and inexperienced River Boards should not be over-strict in relation to local conditions or to the national need to maintain industrial production. No doubt those who drafted the 1951 Act assumed that pollution byelaws would be widely adopted within a few years. Certainly byelaw control was the only means provided for the regulation of existing discharges, but standards proved so difficult to define that none had in fact been confirmed by the time the byelaw principle was cast aside.

The 1951 Act tackled new discharges differently. Each new discharge required the consent of the River Board, the individual consents defining standards of quality and quantity for the effluents. This overcame a flaw in the 1876 legislation – control became anticipatory – and operated sufficiently well on new discharges that the principle of individual consents was extended in 1961 to cover pre-1951 discharges also. The Rivers (Prevention of Pollution) Acts 1951 and 1961 are now superceded by Part II of the Con-

rol of Pollution Act 1974, but individual consents continue as the sole
regulatory device. Periodic review of consents and alteration of their conditions allow progressive improvements in effluent quality.

The problem of defining appropriate standards for discharges and for river
reaches, although perhaps most obvious when uniform byelaw standards
were attempted, still remains. Each discharge can now be judged and
regulated individually, and altered as necessary, and this gives a fair degree
of flexibility, but it is by no means a simple task to determine what are the
proper conditions to attach to a particular consent to discharge.

The most straightforward case concerns a new discharge controlled so
that the quality of the receiving water suffers no significant deterioration.
Just to maintain the *status quo* requires high levels of technical skill and
judgement. Complications arise when a Water Authority desires to improve
the quality of a polluted stretch of river. The authority might like the
improvement to begin with the discharge under consideration, and seek to
impose more stringent consent conditions than have been imposed hitherto.
The prospective discharger, on the other hand, might expect to be dealt with
on the same terms as similar dischargers in the vicinity. A resolution of
this conflict must take some account of the additional costs to the discharger if higher than usual standards are required of his effluent. Indeed,
social costs, including the loss of new employment opportunities, may
occasionally tip the balance in favour of more pollution, a Water Authority
reluctantly agreeing to an industrial discharge which it recognises will
cause a deterioration in river quality, in the hope that once the industry is
established and profitable, improved on-site treatment facilities will correct
the effluent. This emphasises again that water management cannot be discussed in isolation. River quality must be considered in relation to the
multiple demands made on the river, demands deriving from the regional
economy.

Unlike their predecessors, the Water Authorities are directly involved
with the costs of effluent disposal and pollution prevention. The River
Authorities had responsibility for implementing the pollution prevention
legislation but no responsibility for financing or operating treatment works.
Now the Water Authorities have taken over sewage and sewerage functions
from the local authorities, together with many decrepit, obsolete sewage
treatment works in need of immediate capital investment. In the first
financial year of the reorganised water industry, slightly more than half the
Water Authorities' total revenue expenditure was for sewage collection and
disposal and for pollution prevention. Of their capital expenditure, nearly
two thirds went for these activities, a sum of £278 million, indicating the
enormous burden placed on them by previous under-investment (National
Water Council 1975a).

The studies of the Rivers Mersey and Trent which follow illustrate these

two fundamental problems, the definition of water quality standards whic
reconcile the different demands on the river, and the accumulation of fund
sufficient to achieve these standards.

The River Mersey

The River Mersey and its tributaries upstream of the tidal limit at Howle
Weir, Warrington, drain a catchment of 780 square miles, and the pollutio
problem arises from a concentration of population and industry in a regio
of comparatively small streams. The Mersey begins life in the centre c
Stockport, formed by the Rivers Tame and Goyt, each bringing dow
sewage and trade effluent and getting the Mersey off to an unfortunate star
The principal tributary of the Mersey is the River Irwell which drains sout
east Lancashire, north and east of Manchester. Bugler (1972: 41) used th
Annual Reports of the Mersey and Weaver River Authority to paint a horrify
ing picture of industrial cause and effect on the Irwell. It may well be tha
'Manchester is ashamed of the Irwell', fencing it in with warehouses and no
daring to expose open streets on its banks, but upstream industrialists hav
been glad of its services as a trade effluent sewer.

The catchment of the non-tidal Mersey is one of the most intensel
industrialised regions in Britain and supports a population of nearly 2.
million. In the estuary, below Howley Weir, the Mersey receives a secon
massive polluting load from the industries and 1.5 million population o
Lancashire and the Wirral peninsular. The results are evident in many mile
of 'poor quality' or 'grossly polluted' (class 3 or class 4) river in the Merse
catchment (Department of the Environment and Welsh Office 1971), i
anaerobic conditions producing hydrogen sulphide in the upper estuary and
nearer the sea, in lumps of crude sewage and balls of fat deposited on th
foreshore (Porter 1973: 81–2).

As elsewhere, it is the Industrial Revolution in the late eighteenth an
nineteenth centuries that must be blamed for much of the present pollutio
problem. Fishing was an important industry on the Irwell and Mersey int
the early nineteenth century and salmon were still caught in Mancheste
around 1800. Thereafter pollution increased and fishing decreased, and th
last fish were taken from the River Irwell in the 1840s. A fishing industry sur
vived in the Mersey estuary for much longer, well into this century, to b
finally destroyed by pollution in the late 1930s.

The expanding cotton and wool textile industries, particularly the bleach
ing, dyeing and finishing processes, put out large volumes of liquid, highl
polluting wastes, as well as stimulating local production of dyestuffs an
chemicals and hence another source of pollution. Paper making, salt-base
heavy chemical industries and coal-gas manufacturing joined earlie
industrial polluters, as did the waterborne sewage from the rapidly growin
towns which accompanied this industrial success.

Stinking black rivers, devoid of fish life, were eventually the subject of public complaint, and in 1891 the Mersey and Irwell Joint Committee was established, under the provisions of the 1876 Act. The Committee began its work enthusiastically, pressing local authorities to install sewerage and sewage treatment facilities and even bringing legal proceedings against the more dilatory of them. Success was considerable on the sewage treatment front, but less so when the Committee came to tackle the industrialists. The 'best practical means' of preventing pollution from industrial sources were often merely the settlement of solid material and, while better than nothing, settlement did not prevent the discharge of many grossly polluting, high oxygen demanding effluents. The economic depression after the First World War was no encouragement to industrialists to invest in better treatment plants, and then, when the economy revived, the Committee was powerless to control new industries, some of which, making synthetic fibres, discharged particulary noxious effluents (Mersey and Weaver River Authority 1970).

In 1939 the Mersey and Irwell Joint Committee gave place to the Lancashire Rivers Board, then to the Mersey River Board, the Mersey and Weaver River Authority and now the North West Water Authority. Agencies concerned to control pollution thus have a long history, but the Mersey river system shows all too clearly the effects of the regional reluctance to spend money on treatment works for effluents, many of which, it must be admitted, are difficult and expensive to treat satisfactorily.

In its First Annual Report the North West Water Authority revealed the inadequacy of the sewage treatment works it had inherited. When setting terms of consent to discharge the former River Authorities took account of the state of the receiving waters and the probable effects of the particular discharge. As a result consent conditions vary from place to place. Table 4 shows the performance of treatment works of different sizes, compared with the terms of their discharge consents. For a works to be judged satisfactory in this context, 80 percent of the final effluent samples taken will have met the consent conditions and the works will be operating within its

TABLE 4 *Performance of sewage treatment works in the North West region, compared with the terms of their discharge consents*

Actual dry weather flow Ml/d	Satisfactory	Border-line	Unsatisfactory	Bad	Total consented works
over 22.7	1	0	7	7	15
2.27–22.7	12	19	30	32	93
0.27–2.27	23	14	33	26	96
less than 0.27	47	81	51	48	227
Total	83	114	121	113	431

Based on North West Water Authority 1975:37.

design flow capacity. A works judged bad will have less than 20 percent of final effluent samples within the consent conditions and/or be operating at a flow 50 percent in excess of the design flow. The borderline and unsatisfactory categories fall between these two extremes. In addition to the 431 consented works shown, there are another 212 works, mostly very small, operated without consent and so not analysed here.

The numbers in the unsatisfactory and bad categories are staggering, and some of the worst offenders are to be found in the Mersey catchment. The situation is no better when one turns to industrial discharges. In the North West region as a whole, of 206 consented discharges to non-tidal waters, only 49 are classed as satisfactory.

Discrepancies between consent conditions and actual discharges are easy enough to explain but difficult to reduce. Throughout the country urban development has run ahead of the provision of sewage treatment works, new areas of housing being sewered into existing works which, even if generously designed initially, are soon over-loaded. When this happens, some sewage is inadequately treated, while some may escape treatment altogether. The Working Party on Sewage Disposal found that only when the over-load was so great that breakdown was imminent was development stopped until sewage treatment capacity could be extended (Department of the Environment and Welsh Office 1970: 9). The situation today is much the same: the problem of over-loading is severe, but the remedy – increasing treatment capacity – demands capital and land, both of which are in short supply.

The North West Water Authority is currently using portable, package treatment units to extend the most critical works, but this is really a 'fire fighting' exercise to prevent an immediate collapse of the system, rather than a long-term strategy. Paradoxically there is probably enough sewage treatment capacity within the region as a whole, some works having been built large to anticipate future development. One might therefore suggest as an interim policy the redeployment of sewage works, analogous to the redeployment of water sources, with sewage taken from over-loaded works to under-used ones, except that sewers are considerably more expensive to construct than aqueducts. Only a very limited rerouting seems possible.

If new capacity must be installed, the question arises, would regional concentration on a few large plants be preferable to small extensions of many plants. As yet there is no policy of regional concentration for, although there are undoubtedly scale economies to be had in capital and staffing for large units, large works need very large volumes of dilution water and must be sited well down the river system. Small works can discharge to small rivers and benefit from natural purification as the effluent passes downstream. They also gather in their effluent from a smaller area, thereby saving on sewerage costs.

The Water Authority is continuing the policy of the Mersey and Weaver

River Authority of encouraging industrial concerns to discharge their wastes to sewage works rather than direct to the rivers. More and more industries are doing this, and are charged for conveyance and treatment services, including removal of solids, biological oxidation and disposal of sludge. Before an industrial effluent can be accepted for treatment, it must be checked for its effects upon the fabric of the sewers and the health of the men working there, on its possible inhibition of biological treatment by toxics, and on substances which may pass through the treatment works unchanged and be concentrated in either liquid effluent or sludge. Some industrial effluents are unacceptable at treatment works, and must be disposed of by other means, for instance by incineration or dumping on licensed tips.

There are also cases where the firm is able to treat its effluent better itself on-site, where the polluting substances are in higher concentrations and easier to remove. This is often a matter of scale of operation. The larger firms are more likely to be able to build their own specialised treatment plants and to operate them efficiently, disposing of the final effluents directly to the river.

The biggest and most modern sewage treatment works in the region is that at Davyhulme, serving Manchester and the surrounding district. The Davyhulme plant has been extended in stages since 1963, the commissioning of the extensions being evident immediately in large reductions in the BOD of Mersey water as it passes over Howley Weir into the estuary. Both domestic sewage and industrial wastes are treated here, the latter making up about one third the input by volume but two thirds by polluting load (volume times strength). Manchester's effluent is very diverse and gives an opportunity to test a range of treatment techniques, an opportunity taken up by a NATO-sponsored experimental plant for advanced waste water treatment recently completed there. Set up by the NATO Committee for the Challenges of Modern Society, the advanced waste water treatment plant uses precipitation, flocculation and activated carbon techniques, in addition to the conventional biological methods of the main Davyhulme plant, investigating their effectiveness and costs of operation.

Sludge from the Davyhulme works is collected by boat and taken via the Manchester Ship Canal and the Narrows out into Liverpool Bay for dumping. At present the environmental effects of sludge disposal at sea are not fully known. Detailed studies at a sludge dumping ground in the Firth of Clyde suggested a build-up of toxic metals in the bottom mud and of organochlorine compounds in the fauna, the species range of which was much reduced (Mackay and Topping 1970), but effects in Liverpool Bay seem rather different (Department of the Environment 1972). Samples from the dumping ground show very few characteristics of pollution, probably because of currents and bed mobility in this part of the sea. There is little or no opportunity for organic mud to settle. In contrast, at the mouth of the

Mersey estuary, the sea bed fauna show the same concentration on a few species as in the Firth of Clyde, but here arising from river pollution, not sludge dumping. Sludge dumping in Liverpool Bay is increasing, however, and there is a monitoring programme to detect significant ecological changes in the Bay.

The pollution problems of the Mersey estuary differ from those of the non-tidal river. Domestic sewage from most of the urban areas around the estuary is discharged without any form of treatment. Raw sewage from a population approaching one million goes straight into the estuary, there to be joined by industrial effluents from oil refining, a wide range of chemical industries, food processing and paper making–effluents with high oxygen demands and often floating oil and fat as well.

The North West Water Authority is handicapped by a lack of control over the older-established industrial discharges. Tidal rivers and estuaries were at first exempted from the 1951 river pollution controls. Then in 1960 the Clean Rivers (Estuaries and Tidal Waters) Act allowed new, post-1960 discharges to be regulated, but the 1961 river pollution legislation again exempted estuaries. As a result pre-1960 discharges continued uncontrolled, and the Control of Pollution Act 1974, following the recommendations of the Working Party on Sewage Disposal (Department of the Environment and Welsh Office 1970:26) and the Third Report of the Royal Commission on Environmental Pollution (1972:10) sought to put this right. But implementation has been delayed, and Water Authorities' powers to regulate polluting discharges is still incomplete.

Greater control is, in any case, only part of the answer to the Mersey estuary's difficulties. More treatment works are needed, both to deal with crude sewage from the older urban areas of Liverpool and Birkenhead and to improve industrial discharges from the Widnes–Runcorn area and the Wirral peninsular.

In 1971 local authorities, industrialists and water interests set up a Steering Committee on Pollution of the Mersey Estuary which, according to its terms of reference, was to investigate and recommend action:

(a) to ensure that the estuary water should *at all times* contain a sufficient level of oxygen to obviate odour nuisance; and

(b) to obviate the fouling of the River Mersey foreshore and beaches by crude sewage or solids or fats from industrial effluents.

Even such comparatively modest objectives as these, to remove only the most gross and obvious manifestations of pollution, are extremely costly to achieve.

Consulting engineers reported to the Committee in 1974 on alternative shore-line sites for sewage treatment works (Watson and Watson 1974), but more recently the problems of acquiring shore-line sites in Liverpool have turned attention inland to the Liverpool North sewage works, which could be much extended to receive all the city's sewage, brought to it by intercepting sewers. After treatment the final effluent would be taken back again for discharge to the estuary. Estimated costs of treating Liverpool's sewage have risen to over £100 million, and if discharges from the Wirral are included in a more comprehensive plan for cleaning up the estuary, total costs might approach £200 million. The North West Water Authority's capital allocation is currently £68 million a year, most of which is committed to continuing work, with only £7 million a year available for new starts. Such massive schemes are thus impossible on present funding.

The River Trent

The Trent is remarkable among England's larger river systems in having most of its population concentrated near the headwaters. The natural, clean water flow of many of these streams is negligible compared with the discharges of dirty water received from population and industry supplied, for the most part, with clean water from outside the Trent basin. The catchment of around 4000 square miles contains a population in excess of 5.5 million. Nearly half the population lives in the conurbations of Birmingham, the Black Country and Stoke-on-Trent, and the upper Trent and the Tame which drain these areas carry concentrated flows of sewage and industrial effluent – about 95 percent of the low summer flows of the River Tame (Trent River Authority 1972:1). A further source of pollution is surface runoff from highly developed, industrial areas. After a rainstorm the upper rivers may be dirtier, not cleaner, because the added dilution water is contaminated. Downstream the Derwent and Dove tributaries bring in clean water and allow the lower part of the river system to support coarse fisheries. The upper rivers are fishless.

Overall there is a noticeable improvement in water quality downstream, both compared with quality in the upper Trent and Tame and compared with quality a decade or so ago. At Trent Bridge, Nottingham, the average concentration of ammonia was measured as 3.5 parts per million in the period 1962–4, and is now around 0.9 ppm. BOD loadings have been reduced from 14.0 in the early 1960s to 7.3 now. There is a deterioration, however, in the last, tidal section of the River Trent, as it receives seriously polluted water from Scunthorpe via the Bottesford Beck. Sewage and wastes from the steel industry contribute to a reduction in the tidal Trent's dissolved oxygen, and on occasions the river is almost deoxygenated as it enters the Humber estuary.

In the Trent basin, as in the Mersey, industrialists are encouraged to send their effluents to sewage works. Before the reorganisation of the water industry Birmingham and several other local authorities already had sophisticated control and charging schemes for trade effluents. The Severn–Trent Water Authority is rationalising the various local policies and extending trade effluent control to areas formerly without it. But the Water Authority accepts that in certain circumstances an industrialist may be able to treat his effluent better on-site, or at least give it useful pre-treatment before it goes into the public sewers. Each industrial effluent must be considered individually, for its own properties, in relation to effluents already in the sewers and in relation to the treatment processes used at the sewage works.

The grossly polluted state of many reaches of the upper rivers creates special difficulties for the Water Authority. Standards for effluent discharges, whether from sewage works or direct from industry, depend on what each river reach is wanted for – trout fishery or open sewer. Many reaches have long been used as the latter, and this has two consequences. One is that any quality improvement demands extremely strict effluent standards, because the receiving water is presently of very poor quality and affords little or no dilution. The other is that, in the days of the Trent River Authority, both industrialists and local authorities appealed, very often with success, against the proposed consent conditions, on the grounds that the standards were too expensive to comply with or otherwise unreasonable in view of existing discharges and the prevailing state of the river.

Figure 25 seems to imply that, except for the curious case of the River Derwent, the Severn–Trent Water Authority inherited sewage treatment works whose liquid effluents were not greatly at variance with the consent conditions set by the former River Authority. Compared with the North West Water Authority, the Severn–Trent seems to have come off fairly well. Figure 26 shows a different picture. Here the same effluent discharges are very unsatisfactory indeed compared with standards the River Authority originally wanted to impose. The difference between the two figures indicates the revisions consequent upon appeal. However, on the River Derwent the two figures match. This is a relatively clean river on which more normal standards were imposed and, in general, not met.

A memorandum from the Ministry of Housing and Local Government in 1966 discussed the problem of standards for sewage effluents, and suggested that Royal Commission standards be taken as the norm. If a River Authority wished to set standards higher than these, then a special case should be made out. The Ministry also suggested that a sensible course would be to improve all effluents to Royal Commission standards, rather than bring some to a higher standard and leave the rest alone. Such advice was not welcomed by the Trent River Authority for, through the appeals it encouraged, it hindered the Authority's attempts to clean up the most seriously polluted stretches of water.

Since reorganisation has given the Water Authority direct control over sewage treatment works, the matter has been partly internalised. Now only industrialists have the right of appeal against consent conditions. As a check on Water Authority monopoly certain consents for treatment works have to be referred to the Department of the Environment, but it is unlikely that Authorities will be held back from applying strict conditions where they wish to do so. Paying for treatment works from their own funds, the Water Authorities can be expected to look very critically at the costs and benefits of

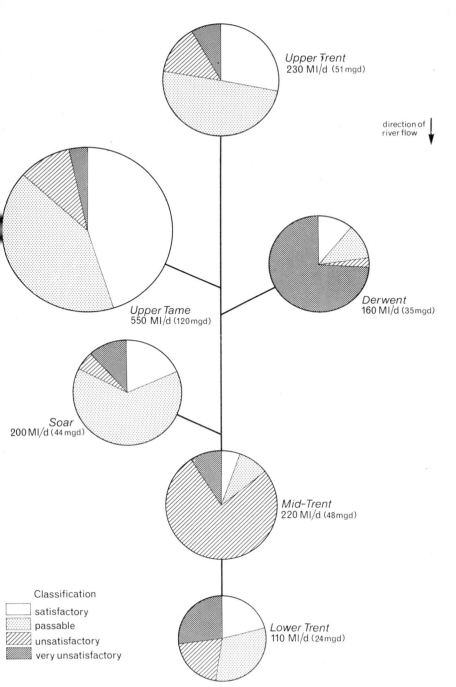

Figure 25   The River Trent: comparison of sewage effluent quality with actual
standards 1973.
Source: Severn–Trent Water Authority 1974b:194.

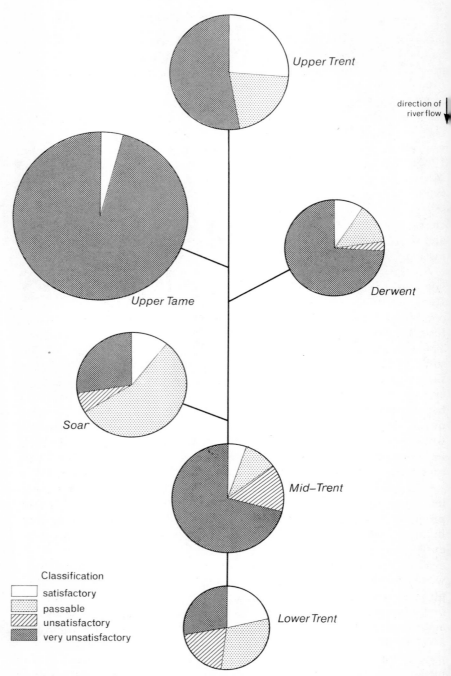

direction of river flow

Classification
☐ satisfactory
▨ passable
▨ unsatisfactory
■ very unsatisfactory

Figure 26   The River Trent: comparison of sewage effluent quality with standards proposed by the former River Authority.
Source: Severn–Trent Water Authority 1974b:195.

different degrees of sewage treatment. In the Trent basin there will probably be highly selective investment, with more than previously spent in certain pollution-sensitive areas and less where natural dilution and self-purification can cope with the present pollution load.

The planning of investment in new effluent treatment facilities could be assisted by the Trent Economic Model, developed by the Local Government Operational Research Unit to compare alternative methods of meeting water demands in the Trent catchment (Water Resources Board 1972d; 1974). The Economic Model was the culminating achievement of the larger Trent Research Programme which involved the Trent River Authority, the Water Resources Board, the Water Pollution Research Laboratory and several other research organisations. The treatment of effluents before discharge and the later reclamation of polluted water both featured prominently, and we have already mentioned the Programme's work on waste water reclamation through artificial recharge.

Another water treatment facility studied was a series of river purification lakes on the River Tame (Lester, Woodward and Raven 1972; Water Resources Board 1972e). The Tame is grossly polluted, fishless for the whole of its length, and it fouls the River Trent from their confluence downstream for ten miles until the River Dove brings in clean water. Water quality in the Tame deteriorates in storm conditions because of the discharge of dirty surface water from the impermeable catchment and the scouring of deposited sludge from the bed of the river. Much higher standards for discharged effluents would not solve this storm runoff problem. The present suggestion, based on experimental work at Elford and Lea Marston, is to pass the whole of the river flow through a series of seven purification lakes, formed in worked-out river gravels. Settleable suspended solids will be deposited in the first lake, the liquid effluent then passing through the further lakes, allowing time for the processes of self-purification to operate (Woodward 1975).

Costs are put at around £6 million and funds are not available for an immediate start to the work. Within a decade, however, one might expect progress in this most critical section of the Trent system. Without some buffering against storm runoff pollution, much of the benefit of current expenditure on effluent treatment will be nullified.

The Trent basin also houses a NATO-sponsored plant for advanced waste water treatment. The purpose of the installation, at Coleshill, is to allow physical–chemical treatment processes to be tested under near full scale operating conditions, in particular to investigate costs. Two different sewages are treated, one almost entirely domestic in origin, the other containing a substantial amount of industrial effluent. Physical–chemical treatment processes are not new: they were used in the last century but were overtaken by developments in biological treatment. Interest in them is reviving because they operate much more quickly and so take up less space and because they are not disrupted by toxic substances in the sewage.

Cleaner water in the Trent system would benefit amenity and fisheries, and there is a further possibility that the Trent might be used as a source of drinking water for Nottingham. This would free existing sources, the River Derwent and groundwater in the Bunter Sandstone, for deployment elsewhere. Recent quality improvements in the middle reaches of the river make this a plausible suggestion, provided that the water is treated by activated carbon to remove any trace organic compounds that may have entered the river from the region's pharmaceutical industries. Indeed a pilot plant at Nottingham is already producing drinking water from the Trent. Development costs for a large scale river reclamation scheme are being compared with those for other water sources, the two major alternatives being surface storage schemes, at Craig Goch in Wales and Longdon Marsh on the lower Severn.

The River Trent discharges into the Humber estuary, where the Severn–Trent shares responsibility with the Yorkshire and Anglian Water Authorities. The three organisations have agreed a programme for increasing the levels of dissolved oxygen in the upper part of the estuary, where the polluting effects of the Yorkshire Ouse and the Trent are aggravated by the presence of solid particles in suspension, known locally as 'warp' and having a high BOD. Unfortunately here again the present financial difficulties of the Water Authorities threaten to postpone the necessary investment for several years. This, together with the delayed implementation of estuary controls under the Control of Pollution Act 1974, means that the proper regulation of water quality in the Humber estuary is still some way off.

Taken as a whole the estuary is not severely polluted. Deoxygenated water in the upper estuary recovers gradually towards the sea, and even the heavy polluting load discharged from the industries of South Humber Bank does not depress oxygen levels here. Other indicators of pollution are more worrying, however. Investigations by the Ministry of Agriculture, Fisheries and Food have suggested that some of the South Humber Bank discharges are directly toxic to fish close to the outfalls. The shallow margins of the estuary at its seaward end are the nursery grounds for young sea fish, and damage by pollutants could thus have repercussions for both estuary and sea fisheries. The Water Authorities, the Ministry of Agriculture and the University of Hull have chemical and biological monitoring programmes (University of Hull/Humber Advisory Group 1974), for though the estuary is by no means as polluted as the Mersey it could nonetheless be in a critical state for its aquatic life.

Large scale works for effluent disposal

The former highly fragmented system of sewage disposal, with its 1400 operating units, gave little opportunity for the large scale planning of sewage services. Only a few plants provided a regional rather than a local service, the Davyhulme works being one. This treats mixed domestic and trade effluent from the Greater Manchester region and accepts sludge from an even wider area, delivered to it by road tanker and then taken, together with Davyhulme's own sludge, out to Liverpool Bay for dumping. The reorganisation permits the planning of many more regional schemes, should these be thought desirable.

The North West Water Authority plans no great regional concentration of treatment capacity in inland areas, beyond that already existing at Davyhulme. Lack of dilution water for the liquid effluents and high costs of re-sewering to a new collection pattern make very large inland treatment works unattractive in the North West. In the estuary and coastal areas the dilution problem disappears, and for the Mersey estuary one or two really big treatment works may well be the answer for sewage and trade effluents at present discharged in an untreated state.

The sea's capacity to receive and disperse pollutants has invited the discharge of much, generally untreated, effluent from coastal areas, and in the last decade or so there have been several proposals to use sea outfalls to get rid of inland-derived effluents also.

In 1965 the Trent River Authority suggested that untreated effluents from Scunthorpe's steelworks be piped across country for discharge into the lower Humber estuary at Killingholme, South Humber Bank, instead of going into the River Trent. The Lincolnshire River Authority, in whose area the discharge could occur, opposed it on the grounds that it would be a hazard to fisheries and would discredit the pressures put on South Humber Bank industrialists to improve their effluents. Then followed a proposal to move the outfall to the open sea, thereby giving the South Humber Bank dischargers an opportunity to link to the pipeline and dispose of their effluents at a distance. At present neither scheme seems likely to be adopted. The long sea outfall proposed for Teesside's intractible industrial effluents (Watson and Watson 1968) has similarly come to nothing, and for the same general reasons. The mixing of effluents from several different industrial sources could be dangerous, and the contributing industrialists would need to exchange a deal of technical information before the safety of the pipeline was assured. Also there is international concern for the state of the North Sea, particularly regarding heavy metals and organochlorine compounds. Domestic sewage may be less of a hazard, provided that tides and currents do not bring it back inshore, and for sewage regional collection schemes and long sea outfalls may well be feasible.

It is also possible to increase a river's capacity to receive effluents, improving its quality while it accepts heavy pollution loads. The purification lakes proposed for the River Tame have this as their purpose. Another form of in-channel treatment is river aeration, to maintain or increase the dissolved oxygen concentration. Individual effluent outlets can be designed so that the discharge passes down a stepped weir, picking up oxygen as it goes, and a whole river can be re-aerated by weirs.

The reorganised water industry is able to deal with pollution problems on a larger scale than previously and to compare the merits of improving effluents at source, improving river quality *in situ*, or diverting discharges from rivers to the sea. Administrative matters have so occupied the Water Authorities in their first years of existence that only now are the wider implications of the change coming to be appreciated. The next few years could produce radical new ideas for regional effluent treatment and disposal.

Instruments of policy: pollution control through discharge consents

The 'consent to discharge' is at the heart of river pollution control in this country, and its efficacy depends on the definition and enforcement of appropriate standards for the effluent. The 1912 Royal Commission 20/30 standard was an early attempt to define 'normal' standards for discharges from sewage treatment works, confirmed by the Ministry of Housing and Local Government memorandum in 1966, but never enshrined as a uniform requirement in the pollution prevention legislation. The Water Authorities are free to set consent conditions that vary according to the individual effluents, the state of the receiving waters and the other uses desired of the river reach, a necessary freedom as the River Trent example has demonstrated.

Another dimension of the problem which demands that consent conditions be alterable as well as variable from discharge to discharge is that the volume of effluent increases year by year. Table 5 below shows, in a hypothetical case, how higher standards of quality are required simply to maintain a constant pollution load and a constant river quality. The calculations assume an increase of 3 percent a year in effluent volume, and begin from Royal Commission standards with a sewage effluent of 20 parts per million BOD diluted with eight times its volume of clean water to give a downstream river

TABLE 5   *Calculated effect of a 3 percent annual increase in effluent volume on downstream river quality*

Year	Effluent:river flow	River BOD ppm	Effluent BOD to maintain downstream river BOD of 4 ppm
0	1:8.0	4.0	20.0
5	1:6.9	4.3	17.8
10	1:6.0	4.6	15.9
15	1:5.1	4.9	14.3
20	1:4.4	5.3	12.9
25	1:3.8	5.7	11.6
30	1:3.3	6.2	10.6

Source: Woodward 1975:12.

BOD of 4.0. If the BOD of the sewage effluent remains the same but its volume increases, river quality deteriorates (column 3). If constant river quality is required, then the BOD of the effluent has to be reduced (column 4).

In 1975 the principle of variable standards was challenged in the councils of the EEC when Community standards for aqueous and gaseous emissions were debated. Standards were to be applied *uniformly* in the Community area, but British objections were sufficiently strong to exempt us from this requirement. The British members argued that our system of control was well-established and effective. Within the water industry at home it was said that British standards, though variable, were in general higher than those likely to be operational within the EEC and that having once tried uniform standards, in the byelaw phase of control, and found them unworkable, Britain should not acquiesce to their revival.

The definition of effluent standards is only half the pollution prevention exercise. They also have to be enforced. Without doubt many effluent discharges, both from sewage treatment works and from industrial premises, fail to meet the consent conditions. The Water Authorities' periodic sampling of effluents and river water helps to pinpoint consent infringements, but legal action against the offenders, although used occasionally, is no panacea. A treatment works or industrial concern must be capable of producing the correct effluent before it can be forced to do so. The practical problem of enforcement is that often the capability is not there: consent conditions do not match the realities of the situation.

The Water Authorities are acutely aware of this at their inherited sewage treatment works, many of which do not and cannot meet the conditions set by the former River Authorities. The Water Authorities are thus offenders and policemen simultaneously. Only after considerable capital expenditure to improve the works will effluents and consents correspond, and in the meantime there is a case for revising the consent conditions downwards so that they more nearly match present effluent qualities. When the Control of Pollution Act 1974 is brought fully into effect, members of the public will be able to take proceedings against a Water Authority if its effluents infringe consent conditions, a check on Water Authority monopoly in the sphere of sewage disposal. This is a spur, if one is needed, for the Authorities to get their own effluents and consent conditions in balance, and thereafter it would seem unreasonable to deny to those industrialists who required it the same downward revision of their consent conditions.

Many consent infringements are explained away with admissions that the original conditions were unrealistic or that urban growth and industrial processes have overtaken them. As long as an infringement is not wilful or negligent, it tends to be condoned by the Water Authorities. A more straightforward approach would be to revise consents and then enforce them strictly, even if this meant an apparent lowering of effluent standards.

If an effluent standard is to be enforceable, it must be appropriate in terms of what the river requires and what the discharger can afford to provide. This is emphasised by the delayed application of the controls possible under the 1974 Act to pre-1960 estuary discharges. Dischargers of presently unregulated effluents argue that they cannot yet afford to make their effluents comply with the type of standards the Water Authorities want to impose, and although the delay may not be as long as the industrialists would like, a delay there is, for economic reasons.

Instruments of policy : pollution charges

The direct control of pollution through consents to discharge functions properly only when consent conditions take account of what the discharger is prepared to pay to treat his effluent. Pursuing the point further and admitting that pollution prevention is predominantly an economic problem, there is a case to be investigated for allowing the price mechanism to regulate pollution. The Royal Commission on Environmental Pollution, in its Third Report (1972), debated the arguments for and against the replacement of consents by pollution charges. The appended minority report by Lord Zuckerman and Professor Beckerman considered the reorganisation of the water industry to be a good moment to make this change, which would give, so the argument ran, a cheaper means of achieving the same amount of pollution abatement. The majority of the Commissioners were more cautious, recommending 'that the Government should forthwith examine the case for adopting a charging system' (p 68), not committing themselves to pollution charges without more inquiry.

American studies reported by Russell (1974) predict individual industries' responses to pollution charges. The minority report regretted the absence of economic studies in this country, but considered the case for adopting charges as the main regulator of pollution already adequately established. It rests on the price mechanism giving an incentive to polluters to reduce pollution to the point where the costs of further abatement would be greater than the damage done by the pollution. Assuming charges are correctly set, polluters bear the true social costs of their operations, but they are free to choose how they bear them – as charges for polluting discharges, or as costs for on-site treatment or recycling to give cleaner or smaller, and hence cheaper, discharges. The price mechanism can produce a given amount of pollution abatement at a lower cost than direct controls, because firms are left to find the most economical way of reducing pollution, and because total pollution abatement is distributed between firms in the cheapest way.

Water abstractors must pay charges, as must dischargers sending their trade effluents to sewage treatment works. The introduction of charges for effluent discharges direct to rivers is a logical step, making a comprehensive charging system for effluents complementary to that for abstracted water.

Proponents of pollution charges admit, however, that direct controls cannot be dispensed with entirely, though ideally their role would be minor. Upper limits need to be set to the amount of pollution that can be tolerated, in each river reach and in each effluent discharge. Licences to discharge are envisaged, stipulating the maximum permitted polluting load and applying a scale of charges for pollution at levels below the maximum.

The water industry was reorganised without the introduction of pollution charges, and a subsequent report on the industry's economic and financial policies (Department of the Environment 1974b), while it discussed trade effluent charges at sewage treatment works, made no mention of charges for direct discharges. Reluctance to move from consents to charges is based on two main reservations. Consents, when properly enforced, guarantee a certain level of water quality, but charges place no obligations on dischargers (except that an upper limit of pollution is prescribed), and thus offer no such guarantee. The other reservation concerns the expertise necessary to fix the charges, an expertise thought not to exist yet.

It is unlikely that the price mechanism alone will ever be allowed to regulate river pollution in this country, but certain elements of the minority report proposals could well be used alongside direct controls. Abstraction licensing and charging already give an example of dual controls over the allocation of clean water. Revenue from pollution charges would surely be welcomed, for the funds remaining after administration costs were deducted could be used to finance in-channel river treatment or other regional schemes. At present the disposal of effluents direct to rivers is one of the very few water services that is free. Consent conditions do indeed force some dischargers to bear costs of on-site treatment but, where dischargers cannot or will not improve their effluents at source, all their pollution costs are passed on to society. Pollution charges would help to redistribute costs and, so long as they were set at levels that more than covered administration, would give the Water Authorities a new source of income so badly needed to finance effluent and river treatment.

CHAPTER 8

SOME NATIONAL ASPECTS OF WATER MANAGEMENT

The water industry in England and Wales has always been decentralised and, for a long time, excessively fragmented. The 1580 water agencies which existed at the moment of reorganisation were already the result of amalgamation, particularly among the water undertakers. Then the Water Act 1973 dealt decisively with the fragmentation problem, but carefully preserved a decentralised form of management in the ten regional Water Authorities.

It has never seriously been questioned that a decentralised system is the right one for the water industry: what we have now seems to have evolved naturally through a process of coalescence of local interests. The general advantages of decentralisation – greater public participation and initiative, more attention to variable local conditions, shorter lines of communication and so on – are complemented by the specific advantages of managing a river basin or group of basins as a single hydrologic entity, and regional Water Authorities based on river basins should reap all these benefits.

Yet the Water Authorities cannot act entirely without regard to each other. The standards of services and the charges made for them can be critically compared by consumers who have a knowledge of more than one region, and public concern about regional variations may be instrumental in reducing them, if not in imposing total uniformity. Coordination is also necessary between those Water Authorities presently transferring water in bulk. The inherited pattern of water sources and supply areas makes some Authorities net importers and others exporters. Complete regional self-sufficiency could, no doubt, be achieved in time, and in aggregate the Water Authorities are predominantly self-sufficient already, about 90 percent of their water being within-region. Nonetheless, significant inter-Authority transfers do occur, and the management system must be able to maintain them until such time as alternative provisions can be made.

But it may be that, far from being reduced, inter-Authority transfers are increased in the future. Higher rainfall and greater possibilities for surface storage will continue to favour the north and west of the country as source areas and, if institutional arrangements do not hinder transfers, it may be that this natural advantage is exploited further.

Another factor drawing the Water Authorities together is the very large scale of some of the potential source developments. Certain projects for inland and estuary storage could, with maximum economy and efficiency, be built large enough to serve several regions simultaneously. With the Water Authorities collaborating in joint schemes, sharing costs and determining operating procedures, water supply would be a national concern, requiring a national water strategy. Not all water services are best provided by large scale works for several regions, however. Effluent disposal, for example, takes advantage of local dilution water, and the scale economies of water supply and effluent disposal are quite different.

Two essentially national issues in the water industry are inter-Authority water transfers with their associated joint source developments, and publicly unacceptable variations between the Water Authorities' charges for their services. If national policies are needed for water transfers and for charging schemes, some national level organisation is needed to formulate them. A third national concern is the appropriate form and function of the national water organisation, its relation to the regional Authorities and to the central government, of which it may or may not be a branch.

These three also happen to be among the liveliest debated and least resolved of the industry's problems. Regional matters are sorting themselves out reasonably well, but the 1974 reorganisation has been noticeably less successful at national level.

A national strategy for water supply

The summer drought of 1976 has revived the idea of a national grid for water distribution. Although the drought was countrywide in terms of much lower than average rainfall, the acute effects were localised in areas where storage capacity was low in relation to demand or where rainfall had been exceptionally meagre. A national water grid to even out these local disparities in supply is an attractive suggestion and one that has been current for nearly two centuries.

In 1801 William Tatham proposed a network of cast-iron water mains and canals linking all the main river basins together, with six hundred steam engines to drive the pumps (1801: 197, 207), and other writers have envisaged different combinations of rivers, canals and aqueducts to move water around the country. Immediately following the 1976 drought the government indicated its interest in establishing a national water supply system, linking wet regions with dry and increasing within-region water movements to overcome local shortages. The term 'national grid' is used, perhaps misleadingly, because a grid for water would be very different from that existing for electricity. While water can, in theory, be moved anywhere by water main and pump, cost considerations preclude the development of an entirely artificial system. Wherever possible water will move in natural channels and under gravity.

We have already noted the beginnings of a regional grid in the North West region, where the reorganisation of the water industry allows redeployment of sources and aqueducts in a much more flexible and extensive supply system. On a larger scale are the inter-regional bulk transfers, for instance from Lake Vyrnwy into Liverpool. Substantial transfers take place already, and more have been proposed for the future. The Water Resources Board report on *Water Resources in England and Wales* contained suggestions for inter-basin transfers across country from central Wales to the Thames, and these are summarised in figure 27.

New or enlarged surface storage capacity in the mountains of central and north Wales would provide water to regulate flows in the Rivers Dee, Severn and Wye, to permit increased downstream abstraction, some of which would be for transfer by tunnel aqueduct across the watersheds into the catchments of the Dove and the Thames. The Dee, Severn and Wye are already regulated over much of their lengths from storage in the headwaters, and the Board's proposals were for more advanced regulation. Because no two catchments are identical in hydrology, they respond in different ways to rainfall variations. The Thames, for example, a predominantly permeable catchment, responds to and recovers from a drought more slowly than does the impermeable upper Severn. Low flows in the Thames may therefore be out of phase with low flows in the Severn, so that peak demands for transferred water do not coincide with peak requirements for regulation of the Severn. The call on headwater storage is spread over time, reducing the amount of storage below what would be needed to support the two river systems separately (Water Resources Board 1973a vol 1: 17).

River regulation and inter-basin transfer need sophisticated operating procedures, especially when several units of regulation storage are involved. While advocating integrated systems of inter-connected regulated rivers, the Board noted that wrong operating decisions are costly, in failure to meet demands for water or to prevent flooding, or in additional pumping costs. The losses through regulation errors may justify new expenditure on hydrometric networks or rainfall forecasting methods, and recent research in the upper Dee catchment has been investigating rainfall and runoff predictions in relation to operating procedures for the regulated river.

The Board's national programme for water supply rested on supplementing the regional resources of the relatively drier, highly populated south east and Midlands by large scale transfers from the wetter, low demand areas of the north and west. The requirement for additional storage, so it was argued, could best be met by enlarging existing reservoirs or, where new construction was essential, by confining it to a small number of large sites, to minimise environmental disturbance.

The Board's report advocated large scale transfers, but soon after publication the idea began to lose favour. Revised forecasts of population increase and economic growth gave lower figures for future water demand, reducing the urgency of some of the development decisions. Following re-

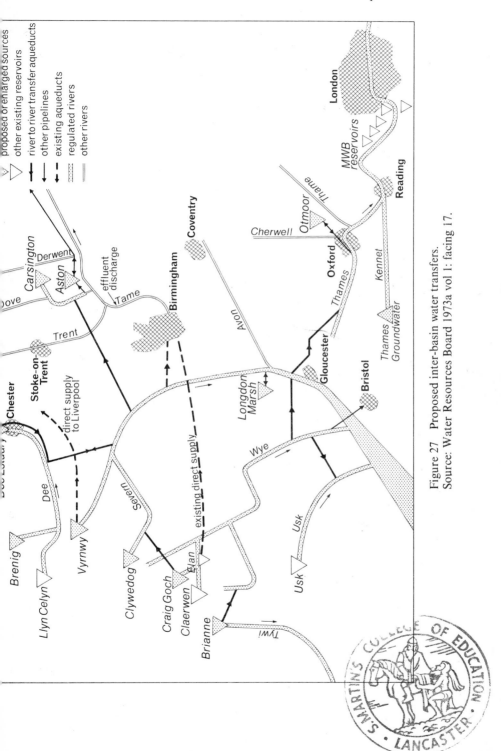

Figure 27   Proposed inter-basin water transfers.
Source: Water Resources Board 1973a vol 1: facing 17.

organisation the more flexible use of regional sources and improvements in effluent treatment and river quality renewed interest in local and regional sources. Then doubts were raised about the terms on which Wales might export more water to England, and these factors combined to lessen the attractions of inter-regional transfers.

The first effects of the reorganisation were to tip the balance in favour of regional self-sufficiency. The Water Authorities 'agreed on the need to avoid constraints on regional transfers where these appear to be more economical' (National Water Council 1975b: 10) but the implication was that the economic calculations would be interpreted from a regional rather than a national point of view. With ten strong, autonomous Water Authorities and comparatively weak organisation at national level, it was to be expected that water development plans would be conceived and optimised regionally, not nationally. As Rydz pointed out immediately before the reorganisation:

A plan which seeks to optimise the pattern of development over England and Wales as a whole necessarily puts considerable strain on any system of independent authorities, whether twenty-nine or ten in number, unless they are provided with a forum in which they can commit themselves to a strategic framework and evolve machinery for operating and financing it effectively [Rydz 1974: 4].

Maybe the National Water Council was intended as such a forum, but the *Review of the Water Industry in England and Wales* (Department of the Environment *etc.* 1976) recognised a failure to provide adequately for national planning and proposed a new National Water Authority to correct this.

Changes in the national organisation and the government's interest in a national water supply system could well bring us back to the Water Resources Board's idea of greater regional interdependence, but only after other management problems have been solved. The Water Resources Board maintained that a few really large source developments are preferable to a proliferation of small ones, but this preference is not shared by all. The appropriate scale of individual developments is a contentious issue. So too are the comparative merits of inland storage, estuary storage, underground storage and desalination. And until the doubts about terms of transfer of water from Wales to England are dispelled, the English Water Authorities are looking closely at their own resources first.

The Craig Goch reservoir enlargement exemplifies problems both of scale and of transfer terms. Craig Goch is the uppermost of a group of direct supply reservoirs in the Elan valley, a tributary of the River Wye, serving Birmingham and the West Midlands. The Water Resources Board recommended as part of the early construction programme an increase in capacity to make it the largest reservoir in Europe. With tunnel links from Craig Goch to the Severn, from the Severn to the Thames, from the Severn to the Dee and from the Wye to the Usk, the enlargement was the centrepiece of the Board's design for river regulation and inter-basin transfer (see figure 27).

Reorganisation took the Elan valley reservoirs away from Birmingham Corporation and placed them with the Welsh National Water Development Authority. For the scheme to operate as the Board proposed, the closest agreement on operation and finance would be needed between the Welsh Authority and the Severn–Trent and Thames Water Authorities, with Wessex involved also, drawing supplies for Bristol from the lower Wye. Early in the discussions the Thames Water Authority indicated its preference for its own source developments – groundwater development for river regulation and new surface storage – and attention focussed on Craig Goch's contribution to the resources of Severn–Trent.

A fundamental difficulty with any really large water resource project is that in the ten or twelve years that may elapse between the formulation of a scheme and its commissioning, overall water demands and their areal pattern will have diverged to a greater or lesser degree from the predicted demands for which the scheme was designed. Flexibility is essential if the commissioned scheme is to serve the new demands, and the Water Resources Board suggested that flexibility could be achieved, even with very large source works, by employing the rivers as the main channels of water distribution. This avoids the extreme rigidity of an aqueduct network, certainly, but it is arguable whether river regulation and transfer, however sophisticated their management, could obliterate major errors in the size or siting of source works.

The Craig Goch scheme started as a proposal for enlargement to enormous proportions. Then, following the effective withdrawal of the Thames Water Authority and the downward revision of estimates of future demand, a scheme for a rather smaller reservoir was promoted.

While schemes of different scales were being considered, the parties fell out over the suggestion of a premium on Welsh water. Soon after reorganisation water charges in Wales increased very rapidly, and some Welsh interests argued that a premium or surcharge on exported water would be a reasonable way of bringing down water charges for Welsh consumers to the level of those in English areas drawing their supplies from Wales (Welsh Office 1975: 44–50). Others contended, more simply, that the water was Welsh, that Wales had a proprietary right to it and should sell it on advantageous terms.

Against the application of a surcharge to supplies drawn direct from the existing Elan valley reservoirs it should be noted that the installations were built and paid for by Birmingham consumers, from whom the reorganisation took them without compensation. The joint development of new or enlarged sources in Wales is a different matter, and agreement is necessary both on cost-sharing of the capital investment and on continuing costs of maintenance, operation and surcharge, if levied. The English Water Authorities in search of more water from Wales are troubled by the whole idea of a surcharge but especially by the possibility that any agreement may be open to revision, that a surcharge may be introduced or varied at any time, in response to political pressures. Talk of Welsh proprietary rights in water led the Severn–Trent Water Authority to withdraw from discussions on the Craig Goch scheme for a time, because of the difficulties of calculating the long-term costs of its involvement in the joint enterprise.

The *Review* considered the surcharge debate and decided firmly that surcharging would prejudice any national water resource strategy, wrongly forcing regions into self-sufficiency. The government's conclusions, that inter-regional transfers should therefore continue as no profit/no loss transactions, seem to have settled the argument for a while, but naturally there is no commitment that future governments will follow the same line.

In November 1976 it was announced that, after resumed talks, the Severn–Trent and Welsh Water Authorities had agreed terms for a Craig Goch expansion. Work is expected to start in 1978 to raise the existing dam and so increase the reservoir perimeter from 5.3 to 21 miles. This is a smaller version of the original proposal but still a very large development by European standards. The Welsh National Water Development Authority will pay one fifth of the capital and running costs, and the Severn–Trent four fifths, water for the Midlands being free of premium or surcharge.

The Craig Goch scheme is part of a general movement away from direct supply to river regulating reservoirs. Greater investment in river regulation schemes makes the efficiency of their operation more important, and with admirable foresight the Water Resources Board devised in 1966 a major research programme to extend present knowledge of the techniques of regulation. The River Dee Research Programme sought to reduce waste of reservoir storage capacity, for instance in unnecessary releases because of inaccurate forecasts of tributary inflow downstream. Long-term and short-term critical period control strategies were developed in a generalised model applicable to the River Dee system (Jamieson 1972).

Another Dee-based research project of fundamental significance is the development of a weather radar system for the measurement and eventual forecasting of rainfall. Areal rainfall is usually determined by interpolating between a number of point measurements at raingauges. Radar can take measurements over a wide area from a single instrumental site, although at present accuracy is improved if the radar is calibrated against a raingauge value within the area of rainfall. The Dee Weather Radar Project is assessing the problems of measuring areal precipitation and of using radar forecasting in a practical way for river regulation (Grinsted 1974; Water Resources Board, Meteorological Office and Plessey Radar Ltd. 1973).

Other types of source development can circumvent some of the problems of inland storage, river regulation and inter-basin transfer just discussed, but not without creating their own. Wherever possible groundwater resources are being developed more fully, for the exploitation of natural underground storage has obvious environmental advantages over the provision of artificial storage on the surface. Management of groundwater resources is not easy, however, and as underground and surface supplies are increasingly inter-linked, operational problems can become extremely complex. The storage of water at estuary sites is another possibility, seriously investigated for nearly two decades, and there are suggestions too for the desalination of sea water.

The early proposals for estuary storage envisaged barrages across the river mouths, to hold back fresh water in shallow lagoons many times more extensive than any inland reservoirs. Objections came thick and fast, from peripheral landowners over problems of land drainage, from navigation interests concerned about access and siltation, and from numerous environmental groups concerned for fisheries, birdlife and other aspects of amenity. *Morecambe and Solway Barrages*, a report on desk studies for these structures (Water Resources Board 1966b), was the last to use the term 'barrage'. 'Estuary storage' was substituted instead, and the new term represented a changed view, of storage at the margins of an otherwise unaltered estuary.

The possibilities for storing fresh water in estuaries are thus two-fold. A barrage can turn the whole or a large part of an estuary into a freshwater lagoon filled directly by the rivers flowing into it. Embanked or 'bunded' reservoirs, on the other hand, occupy a smaller area and hold deeper water, and their filling by pumping from the non-tidal rivers can be closely controlled. In 1967 consultants reporting on storage in the Dee estuary (Ministry of Housing and Local Government 1967) rejected a barrage in favour of bunded reservoirs because they are less difficult to build; dredged sand bunds are relatively cheap to construct; expenditure can be staged; river pumping gives better control over quantity and quality of water stored; and problems of land drainage, navigation and environmental disturbance are reduced, though not necessarily solved. The barrage idea has now been dropped.

Even so, estuary storage in bunded reservoirs is a course to be pursued with caution. The Water Resources Board (1973a vol 1: 49) recommended the development of only one estuary at a time, so as to confine the initial technical and ecological problems, both likely to be considerable. The Dee estuary seems the most probable for early development, with Morecambe Bay and the Wash as additional contenders.

The flow of the River Dee is already regulated by discharges from Llyn Celyn and the new Brenig reservoir. If the operation of the upstream and downstream storages was coordinated, unnecessary regulation releases in the headwaters could be taken into storage in the estuary, making the whole Dee system more efficient. But the Dee estuary is internationally important as the habitat of wading birds, and this and other environmental considerations must be weighed against the demands to alter the margins of the tidal flats. Estuary storage destroys no farming land, and land drainage and navigation interests can probably be accommodated at reasonable cost. It is the estuary habitat of fish and birds that is most endangered, and in ecological terms estuary storage may be more destructive than the continued development of sites inland.

The desalination of sea water could perhaps be an alternative to the further development of fresh water resources. Britain's long, indented coastline brings large volumes of sea water close to many centres of population, and the process of multi-stage flash distillation (MSF) is capable of transforming the sea into drinking water. The Water Resources Board published two reports on desalination in 1969 and 1972, and development work continues on a number of different processes, some using distillation, some freezing, some reverse osmosis. Indeed British firms are regularly building desalination equipment for foreign markets.

Costs of operation in this country are off-putting, however. In the most favourable circumstances reviewed in 1973 (Water Resources Board 1973a vol 1: 12) the costs of desalted water at source were from 2.5 to 15 times as much as water from conventional sources, and capital costs per unit of output were also several times higher. Between 1969 and 1973 the estimated costs of water from desalination increased more than costs of water from conventional sources, and since 1973 desalination costs have risen further, mainly due to increasing energy prices. Thermal desalination processes, of which MSF is one, are very big energy consumers. Power processes, including secondary refrigerant freezing and reverse osmosis, have lower energy demands and are less sensitive to energy prices, but their capital costs tend to be higher.

In 1973 the Water Resources Board foresaw no major contribution from desalination but allowed that in south east England, where the costs of conventional sources are greatest, desalination might have some practical potential in small applications, perhaps in conjunction within an existing source. Some of the changes since then confirm this pessimism, though not surprisingly the 1976 drought has reawakened interest. The second desalination report (Water Resources Board 1972f) advised against a major programme of research and development, but if it should later appear that the present run of dry years is not a random occurrence but a significant climatic change, then desalination might again warrant serious study. A national water programme needs to encourage research into the technical and economic aspects of new types of water source, against the day when conventional sources are exhausted or out-priced.

National economic and financial policies

The varying regional endowment of existing and potential water sources makes water supply a matter of national as well as regional concern: hence our discussion of a national water supply strategy. Regional variations in the costs of water services likewise make paying for water a national issue.

Following the Water Act 1973 the water industry is required to pay its way without government subsidy, each Water Authority setting its charges to consumers so that income meets outgoings, taking one year with another. Charging policies must, after a period of adjustment up to 1981, show no undue preference to or discriminate against any class of consumer – that is, must appear equitable. In the past different charging principles were applied by the various water companies, local authorities and River Authorities, and an early task for the Water Authorities was the partial rationalisation of the inherited tariffs, increasing them where necessary to maintain income when the contribution from rates was ended. This process of within-region equalisation highlighted between-region variations in the costs of water services and led to demands that equalisation be extended beyond Water Authority boundaries in a national charging policy.

One cause of variation is the loss of rate support for water supply, previously irregularly distributed. Over the whole country sewerage and sewage disposal were charged to the general rates: now the Water Authorities collect their own revenue to offset their new financial responsibilities for sewage services. Water supply, on the other hand, was not everywhere assisted from the rates, but where it was, as in areas of Wales, water supply charges increased very substantially after reorganisation. Water service charges are now separate from the rating system and no longer attract rate support grants from the central government.

While it may have a considerable impact on individual bills, the adjustment of charges after the loss of rates income is no more than a change in the method of payment. More fundamental are the variations in charges which reflect real differences in the costs of providing the services. For instance, physical circumstances favour some regions in water sources, giving them abundant rain and plenty of sites where water can be stored comparatively cheaply. Yet if the population to be supplied from these sources is geographically dispersed over difficult terrain, costs of distribution are high. Assuming no other complicating factor, areas of compact population drawing their water from upland sources will face the lowest costs, even if the sources are distant.

Another cause of variation is the magnitude of the Water Authority's inherited debt. Where an area invested early in its source works or sewage treatment plants, borrowing at a low rate of interest, the debt may already be paid off. Where capital investment was late and at higher interest rates the Water Authority takes on a heavy financial burden, which is further increased as new capital works are undertaken.

The water industry is borrowing very heavily, and compared with other public utilities and industries has a low self-financing ratio. Much of the capital budget, financed by borrowing, is for renewal and replacement, rather than for new development, but ideally renewal and replacement should be funded from income, by setting aside a substantial sum for depreciation of present assets. Those Water Authorities with older (and originally cheaper) capital works are allowing less for depreciation than are those with more recent works, since all put aside the same percentage of the book value of thier assets. Clearly the former's future replacement needs will be greater: the advantages of earlier investments and smaller debts do not last for ever. If realistic allowances for depreciation are to be made, as the National Water Council has urged (1976: 4–5), the presently low-depreciating, low-charging Water Authorities will have to increase their charges, so narrowing the gap between them and the high-depreciating, high-charging Authorities.

The diversity of tariffs taken over by the Water Authorities reflected differences in local costs, some 'real' in physical terms, some less 'real' and due to inherited debt, and others caused by rating differences. Yet it can be argued that it is reasonable to expect similar charges for similar services within each Water Authority region, and certainly a part of the variation can be explained away as historical accident. Each Water Authority has effected some equalisation of charges, in recognition of these arguments, although the extent and speed of equalisation vary from one to another. Certain Water Authorities hold the view that charges should continue to reflect the relative cheapness or high cost of water services at particular localities, since this encourages a more efficient use of resources. The equalisation applied in some regions is thus more qualified than in others.

For example, the Welsh National Water Development Authority moved very quickly towards uniform levels of charges for water supply and sewage disposal (general services), completing equalisation in the financial year 1975–6. The Southern Water Authority is phasing the levelling of its general service charges over a period up to April 1979. Severn–Trent has decided that the same general service charges are appropriate over the entire region, but North West acknowledges significant cost differences in sewage disposal between inland and coastal areas and therefore maintains separate charging divisions.

In some regions, household bills for water supply and general services differ only with the rateable value of the property (since charges are levied on rateable value): in others variability is very much greater, depending on rateable value, charging division, and distance along the Water Authority's chosen road to equalisation.

Internal equalisation is, at varying speeds, reducing within-region variations, but it is also exposing between-region variations previously masked by a plethora of local tariffs. In the financial year 1975–6 average household bills for water supply and general services together ranged from about £23 in the Northumbrian Water Authority region to about £35 in the Southern, South West and Welsh National Water Authorities. Average household bills for water supply alone showed a greater range: from £11 in the Thames Water Authority to £19 in the Welsh National Water Development Authority (Department of the Environment *etc.* 1976: 21).

Consumers in Wales face rather higher bills than most English consumers and, partly because internal equalisation was effected early in the Welsh National Water Development Authority area, the increased water charges made a great impact on public opinion. While phased changes were taking place elsewhere, Welsh consumers had suddenly to shoulder the full burden of the new financial system unsupported by the general rates. The result was that the price of water in the WNWDA area increased on average by 121 percent between 1973–4 and 1974–5, with a corresponding average increase in England of 40 percent (Welsh Office 1975: 7).

Welsh complaint has centred on the extent of the increases in water charges, on the low cost at which the English Authorities take water from Wales, and on the territory covered by the Welsh Authority which, being river basin defined, does not correspond exactly to the Welsh national area. These and related issues were explored by a Committee of Inquiry under the chairmanship of Sir Goronwy Daniel. The Daniel Committee's report recommended early action to reduce the 'excessive' differences in average charges for water between the Welsh and English Water Authorities: 'goodwill is threatened if the inhabitants of the water supplying areas see themselves paying more for their water than consumers in the receiving areas. This is so even though there are good reasons why unit costs of supply are lower in the latter' (Welsh Office 1975: 61).

Significantly higher than average charges are not confined to Wales, however, and though the Welsh case is much publicised, not least for its links with nationalist feeling, there are wide variations in England also. The *Review* proposed a form of inter-regional equalisation to reduce the grosser inequalities between all ten of the Water Authorities, and the Water Charges Equalisation Act 1977 puts this into effect.

Proponents of inter-regional equalisation emphasise the cost variations resulting from accidents of price levels and interest rates at the different times at which works were built, arguing that it is unfair to perpetuate these accidental variations. On the other hand, against equalisation must be set the possible misallocation of resources when the direct link between costs and charges is lost. The *Review*, admitting that charges should be seen to be fairly distributed, nonetheless refused to abandon the principle that each Water Authority should be answerable for its expenditure to the consumers it serves, and the scheme implemented through the 1977 Act is a relatively mild form of equalisation.

It aims only at narrowing the range of average domestic charges for water supply. General service charges are excluded, as are charges for metered water supplies (mainly to industry and agriculture). Now that all water services are provided by the same agency, one can foresee the day when water supply and general services will be covered by a single bill. Therefore it is reasonable to consider equalisation of both charges, but the *Review* found the case for equalising the general service charge less strong, largely because standards of sewage treatment and river quality vary between Water Authorities. Likewise the case relating to metered water supply was thought weaker than that for unmetered, domestic supply, since to some extent at least the metered consumer can influence the size of his bill by economies of use. The unmetered consumer can have no such influence.

Equalisation is therefore confined to unmetered supplies, and is concerned primarily with those parts of the charges deriving from historic debt and depreciation allowance. Other costs involved in water supply will be allowed to vary normally. Over time one might expect the scheme to have a decreasing effect, as variations in historic debt and depreciation worth themselves out of the system.

The government is committed to the principles that any funds needed for redistribution among the Water Authorities should not come as external subsidies from the Exchequer nor be generated by surcharging on transferred water. Funds for redistribution will come from an equalisation levy on those Water Authorities and water companies whose 'relevant financing costs' are below average, this to be determined by the Secretary of State for the Environment. Levies are payable to the National Water Council, for allocation as equalisation payments to Authorities and companies with higher than average 'relevant financing costs'. Both levy and payment are to be passed on in full to consumers, in the form of increased or reduced charges.

One may ask, perhaps, why inter-regional equalisation is on this comparatively modest scale, when internal equalisation is going ahead well. If equalisation is feasible and justifiable at regional level, why this apparent hesitation at national level? Indeed it seems illogical to accept pro-equalisation arguments at one scale and not at another, until one considers the areas of financial responsibility. Whereas the divisions within a Water Authority do not have their own separate financial responsibility, the Water Authorities do. The 1973 Act created them as self-regulating, self-financing organisations, directly accountable to their consumers for the way they collect and use their operating funds. Accountability imposes a salutory financial discipline and also safeguards the autonomy of the Water Authorities. Very extensive inter-regional equalisation, with levies and payments assessed by the Department of the Environment and administered by the National Water Council, would inevitably decrease the Water Authorities' control over their financial affairs, and independence might be lost in other spheres as well. Regional autonomy and regional accountability go together.

A national organisation for the water industry

The debates continue over inter-regional equalisation of charges, inter-regional water transfers, joint source development and common policies on a host of more minor topics, with the National Water Council acting as a sounding board for much of the Water Authorities' discussion. The Council's publications *Views of the National Water Council on the Report of the Water Resources Board* (1975b) and *Paying for Water* (1976) show its dual role, making its own independent statements as well as collecting individual views and defining their areas of agreement. Its statement on depreciation, for instance, could be an important contribution to the development of sound financial policies in the industry, and is unlikely to have come from the regional Authorities.

The weakness of the national organisation – for weakness there is – results not from any inactivity on the part of the National Water Council but from the limits set to its involvement in research and planning. Chapter 2 has shown the fragmentation of former Water Resources Board responsibilities among the National Water Council, the Water Research Centre, the Water Data Unit and the Central Water Planning Unit. In particular the separation of the National Water Council and the Central Water Planning Unit is unfortunate, for both have interests in formulating a national water policy compatible with the plans of the individual Water Authorities. The National Water Council is in the better position to understand Water Authority points of view, since each Authority is represented in its membership, but the Central Water Planning Unit has the broader base of national water data and technical expertise.

The Water Resources Board as it was originally constituted could not survive in the reorganised industry. Some change in the central organisation was necessary for two main reasons. The Board's concern for water *resources*, for source development and bulk transfer, was too narrow. The 1973 Act emphasised water *services* and this change, especially as it concerned effluent disposal and pollution prevention, would have necessitated a widening of the Board's brief. Not an insurmountable obstacle, one might think, for already the Board was becoming involved with water quality issues, regardless of its strict terms of reference, for example in the Trent Research Programme. The other reason, less tangible, was probably the dominant.

Relations were sometimes strained between the Board and the Department of the Environment, between the independent, statutory body and the central government department to whom that body was reporting. Two different arguments came from the Department of the Environment against the Wilson Committee's recommendations to expand the Water Resources Board into a National Water Authority: that with much larger and stronger regional authorities a strong central authority was no longer required;

and that a central authority with wider responsibilities than the Water Resources Board might overlap or conflict even further with central government. Jointly they were responsible for the diminution of the activities of independent national institutions and the increase in central government activity.

Contrary to the first argument, however, the birth and first firm steps of the Water Authorities have not done away with the need for an integrated national water organisation. The individual regional units are functioning well, but still there are matters on which a national perspective is needed, as the *Review* recognised:

The new system was thus designed to enable water resources to be managed comprehensively at river basin level. It did little, however, to ensure that the combined policies and operations of the authorities provide the most effective or economical answer to needs seen in the national terms. Nor did it provide an adequate framework for the national planning necessary to meet such an objective. Given that the water industry is one of Britain's largest ... the lack of adequate central guidance and monitoring to ensure that it operates in the national interest must be regarded as a major deficiency [Department of the Environment *etc.* 1976: 4].

Central guidance could, of course, come direct from central government and the major deficiency be corrected by a further concentration of activity in the Department of the Environment. The *Review*'s proposals for the National Water Authority chose the alternative of 'putting out' the problem to an independent body which would advise Ministers on the one hand and Water Authorities on the other.

The proposals for the National Water Authority are the reverse of the government's earlier thinking about national water institutions. Many individuals in the industry have always maintained that the destruction of the Water Resources Board was misconceived, and the suggested amalgamation of the National Water Council, the Water Research Centre and the Central Water Planning Unit admits that some Board-like institution is needed, integrating research, demand forecasting, development planning and policy formulation. A first priority is the creation of 'a strong national authority, empowered to undertake strategic planning and to ensure that the combined operations of the water authorities accord with national needs and objectives' (Department of the Environment *etc.* 1976: 4).

What explanation can be offered for this *volte face*? The interval between the implementation of the 1973 Act and the publication of the *Review*, less than two years, was scarcely long enough to reveal much of substance that was not evident or predictable before reorganisation. Experience, therefore, is not the major explanation. The government which framed the 1973 Act was Conservative, whereas that which conducted the *Review* was Labour, but it is difficult to advance any straightforward ideological explanation either. The reorganisation and the increased water service charges which accompanied it caused alarm in many quarters, and the promise of review, made by the new Labour Secretary of State for the Environment in June 1974, was political rather than party political. More rewarding might be a consideration of the personal influences and interactions involved, but this is hazardous territory to explore.

One of the duties of the National Water Authority, it is proposed, will be to prepare a long-term national water strategy, a corporate plan for the industry for a twenty-year period setting out a range of options in each policy field, and not so very different from what the Water Resources Board produced within its more limited brief. Once a national strategy is devised and endorsed by Ministers, the regional plans of the Water Authorities will be reviewed against it, and where the regional plans diverge, the National Water Authority will be empowered to require amendments. This is power the Water Resources Board was denied. The Board's recommendations never received the stamp of Ministerial approval, neither did the Board have any authority to interfere with River Authorities' or water undertakers' plans.

A further power to be conferred on the National Water Authority is the reserve power to initiate, promote and require the implementation of proposals central to the national strategy. The Wilson Committee recommended the reserve power to acquire, construct and operate schemes of national significance (Central Advisory Water Committee 1971: 72–3), but the suggestion here, similar in many of its effects, will leave costs and manpower problems to be solved by the Water Authorities.

Schemes which could be counted as of national significance include the Craig Goch enlargement and the Dee estuary storage, and the National Water Authority might adjudicate disputes and facilitate cooperation between the potential participants even without the reserve power being activated. It remains to be seen, however, just what membership and powers the new institution will have. The national creations of the Water Act 1973 came as something of a shock because they bore so little relation to the Wilson Committee's recommendations. While improbable, it is not impossible that the same could happen again.

Also uncertain are the precise implications of devolution to Wales. The Government's devolution proposals (HMSO 1975) provide for transfer of responsibility for water services to the Welsh Assembly, with the Welsh National Water Development Authority and the Severn–Trent Water Authority answerable to the Assembly for their operations in Wales. This arrangement appears to meet the criticisms summarised by the Daniel Committee, that the territory of the Welsh Authority does not correspond to that of the Principality. If the devolution proposals are implemented as they stand, the Assembly will be responsible for the all-Wales aspects of water policy. Over matters concerning both England and Wales, the National Water Authority will consult the Assembly before its recommendations are submitted for Ministerial approval. But with both these institutions – the Welsh Assembly and the National Water Authority – yet to be set up, much is open to alteration. The forces for devolution, active in the English regions as well as in Scotland and Wales, may oppose a greater concentration of power in a National Water Authority, and it is premature to guess at the working links that will eventually, through conflict and compromise, come to connect the centre and the regions.

CHAPTER 9

EVALUATION

The reorganisation of water services has been a protracted affair. The Wilson Committee reported in 1971, the Water Act was passed in 1973 and implemented the following year, and in 1976 the water industry's operation under the new system was reviewed and further changes proposed. Reorganisation and review drew the industry into a morasse of administrative detail, and the drought, coming close on the heels of the *Review*, was in one sense at least a very welcome change, directing the industry's energies outwards again.

The drought was a severe test of post-Water Act arrangements, in the industry's responses both to the immediate problem of providing water when resources were very low and to the long-term problem of planning future water services. Popular demands evident in letters to the press were for much more water storage and bulk transfer, so that such a situation of scarcity never arose again. It is one of the industry's tasks to determine the cost of this strategy and to compare it with alternatives of rationing or recycling. The National Water Council's report *The 1975–76 Drought* has already indicated that massive new investment in source works and distribution networks is unnecessary, given the Water Authorities present capabilities for flexible management. It concluded that to invest heavily at margins of security beyond those demonstrated in 1976 would not make economic sense.

Of course the reorganisation was not effected specifically to cope with extreme conditions, and it would be unfair to judge the water industry solely by its performance during the 1976 drought. This would be to ignore the industry's 'normal' operations and to emphasise water supply above all other water services. The six criteria of water management set up in chapter 1 give a broader base for evaluation.

Does the system allow integrated management of all aspects of water use?

The Water Authorities are river basin-based, an essential for meeting this first criterion. Administrative boundaries correspond to hydrologic boundaries, and this enables the rivers to be managed by one authority from source to mouth. Obviously it would be possible to group individual river basins in patterns different from those of the ten Water Authorities but equally valid from a hydrologic point of view. The present grouping establishes a new unity in some of the main consuming areas, for example in London and the Midlands conurbations, bringing together the former Thames and Lee Conservancies and the Trent and Severn River Authorities, but while the grouping is sensible it is not sacrosanct.

Nor is there anything new in river basin authorities; these date from 1930 and the Land Drainage Act. Rather the achievement of the Water Act 1973 is in the transfer to them of responsibility for all the different water services. The Water Resources Act 1963 advanced the cause of integrated river management, but the River Authorities it created were often only junior partners with the statutory water undertakers and local authorities who had control of water supply and the treatment and disposal of sewage. A River Authority could fulfil neither its water conservation nor its pollution prevention functions really adequately because of this division of authority.

Now the partners have come together in a single organisation. The Water Authority has powers for land drainage and flood prevention, fisheries, water conservation and pollution prevention, carried forward from the River Authority, and powers for water supply and sewage treatment and disposal transferred from organisations which do not take the river basin as their base.

It is here that one can perhaps best appreciate the magnitude of the change in management. Capital works for water supply and sewage treatment quite outclassed River Authority works for flood prevention or river gauging, and revenue expenditure by the statutory water undertakers and local authorities on their particular water services was similarly much greater. The major water services – water supply and sewage treatment and disposal – were arranged physically and financially without reference to river basins. Now, in effect, the junior partner has bought out the senior partners. The new river basin organisation has acquired assets and responsibilities many times greater than those carried forward from the old.

The convergence of functions upon the river basin organisation seems natural enough: it recognises more fully than before the essential unity of the hydrologic system. But it is recognition maintained in the face of considerable opposition. The *Review* reaffirmed the principle of integrated river management, but both during the passage of the Water Bill through Parliament and during the period of the review there were doubts that the principle would survive. At one time it seemed quite likely that the authorities proposed in the Water Bill would lose their powers to the local authorities, themselves undergoing reorganisation. In view of the local authorities' investment in water services, directly in sewage treatment and indirectly through the statutory water undertakers, this was a most plausible alternative.

When the Water Act emerged, the river basin organisation came through with it, and local authority interests were accommodated in majority re-presentation in the membership of the Water Authority governing boards. Majority representation on a governing board is a very different thing from direct control, of course, and there was still pressure on the government to increase local authority involvement. Recent bitter feeling between central government and local authorities over financial matters seems to have weakened the latter's chances of winning back direct control of the water services, and the Water Authorities are in a comparatively strong position, having managed their own financial affairs, and the drought, reasonably well.

The new organisation has thus acquired management responsibilities for all the water services drawing upon rivers and aquifers. The water com-panies, the only type of statutory water undertaker to preserve a separate identity after the reorganisation, preserve little more than this, and in effect are operated as units of the Water Authorities under agency agreements. They are likely to disappear into the Water Authorities within the next few years. The control of the canal system, presently with the British Waterways Board, is also under consideration at the moment, and a merging of the British Waterways Board with the proposed National Water Authority is one possibility for integrating navigation more closely with other water services.

Can the management unit apply the full range of management techniques?

Integrated management is possible, and whether a Water Authority achieves this depends on the management techniques available to it. Our second criterion is the Water Authority's ability to use the techniques grouped in chapter 1 as water management information, resource development, re-source allocation and recycling.

The Water Resources Act 1963 enabled the former River Authorities to collect essential information on water resources and abstractions, and the Water Act 1973 added little to regional capabilities. The statutory water undertakers' expertise in demand forecasting has been carried forward to the Water Authorities, and on the sewage disposal side the Water Authorities have rather better information now that they operate the treatment works themselves, but one can point to no substantially new source of data. Any improvement in water management information comes from the bringing together and standardisation of the different data groups.

The allocation of water among potential users also continues much as before, controlled by administrative means, by licences for water abstrac-tions and consents for effluent discharges. In principle the procedures for issuing licences and consents are unchanged by the reorganisation, but in practice the Water Authorities find themselves both the licensing agency and the licensee, where they have taken on simultaneous functions of River Authority and water undertaker or River Authority and sewage authority.

It falls to the Department of the Environment to check in these cases that the Water Authority does not misuse its powers.

Chapters 4 and 7 have considered the possibilities of replacing administrative allocation entirely or in part by economic allocation. The charges at present levied on abstracted water are not designed to influence allocation patterns. The abstraction licences and not the charges associated with them continue as the controlling factor in water allocation.

There are very much more significant changes in the river basin organisation's powers for resource development and for recycling. Chapter 3 has traced some of the implications of the transfer of ownership of water sources from the statutory water undertakers to the Water Authority, in the new possibilities for source redeployment, river regulation and conjunctive use with other sources. Chapter 7 has indicated new possibilities in effluent treatment and disposal which could increase the reuse potential of discharged water and so add to resources. Source development, effluent treatment and in-channel water uses, under the control of the same authority, can be planned together in ways that produce a greater quantity of usable water from the same hydrologic input. The real improvement in resource development techniques is not the discovery of new water sources but the management of existing resources in more productive ways.

The Water Act also allows the industry to make good a long-standing deficiency in the recycling function, by integrating the disposal or rehabilitation of waste water with other water services. This has implications both for improving water quality *per se* and for supporting a range of in-channel and abstractive uses. For resource development and recycling the Water Authorities are much better equipped than were their predecessors.

Is the size of the unit such as to accommodate hydrologic interdependencies and to effect economies of scale?

Reorganisation has put ten Water Authorities in place of 1580 former units or, in territorial terms, ten Water Authorities in place of twenty-nine River Authorities, making the management unit bigger than it has ever been. The reasons for thus enlarging it were to meet the two points above – to contain more of the hydrologic links within the unit, and to increase financial resources so that, where necessary, bigger schemes can be undertaken. The most obvious hydrologic interdependencies are within the river basin. What is taken out of a river or put into a river upstream has effects upon users downstream. Any management unit which deals with the whole of a river basin can accommodate these interdependencies. The Thames Water Authority is such a unit, its territory defined as the basin of the River Thames, with the simplest and most easily justified of Water Authority boundaries.

When river basins are small, as for example those draining south to the

English Channel, other types of hydrologic linkages have to be considered as well. It is probable that a major consuming area will draw water from a basin other than that in which it is situated, or from several basins simultaneously. The separate management of each small catchment could still accommodate upstream/downstream interests, but could not deal with supply and demand patterns which overlapped the watersheds. The grouping of basins for management purposes needs to establish a closer correspondence between the areas of water source, use and return.

The Water Authorities are river basin units, and so upstream/downstream interdependencies are automatically accommodated. Yet only the Thames Water Authority comprises a single basin. The other nine are basin groupings, the Southern, for instance, with many small river systems and the Severn–Trent with two very large ones.

Several bulk water transfers formerly between separate management units are now reduced to within-unit movements. The transfer of water from the Ely Ouse over the watershed to the Essex rivers, mentioned in chapter 5, was formerly a transfer from the Great Ouse River Authority to the Essex River Authority. Now it is a transfer within the Anglian Water Authority. Manchester's Lake District sources were formerly in the territory of the Cumberland River Authority, and the water was moved for use and return in the area of the Mersey and Weaver River Authority. Now the North West Water Authority is able to manage source, use and return of Lakeland water within a system for the whole of the north west region. Even more striking, perhaps, is the union of the Severn and Trent catchments, a union founded on patterns of source, use and return in the Midlands conurbations. Many Midlands consumers, situated astride the watershed, take their water from sources in the Severn and discharge it after use to the Trent and its tributaries. Management of this extended hydrologic system is possible for the first time.

However, many other Midlands consumers take their water not from the Severn but from the Wye, a catchment belonging to the Welsh National Water Development Authority. Nor do all consumers in the North West Water Authority region get their supplies from the north west. Liverpool still draws direct supplies from the upper Severn, as it did last century. Large though the management units are, they are not large enough to bring source and consumer together in all instances. There remain important hydrologic links between the Water Authorities.

Altering the boundaries could reconnect Birmingham consumers with their sources in the upper Wye or link Liverpool with the upper Severn, but this would be at the expense of severing other consumer/source links. The present division of territory between the ten Water Authorities is not perfect. It may not even be the best of all possible divisions, but its general faults would be shared by them all.

The other question related to size is whether the unit is able to effect economies of scale, and again one can point to both significant improvements and defects that remain. It is in the sewage treatment and disposal services that the greatest improvements can be seen, a direct result of the enlargement of the operating unit and of the inclusion of sewage services with other water services. Chapter 7 has indicated new possibilities for improving effluents at source, improving river quality *in situ*, or diverting discharges from rivers to the sea, some of the proposed schemes being on a much larger scale than was possible previously. Nevertheless, the scale economies are such that even the largest treatment or disposal schemes are well contained within the Water Authority boundaries, except in the estuaries that are divided between Authorities.

As chapter 8 has shown, water supply can be different. Proposals for new source works include schemes that might serve several Water Authorities together. Individual management units are not large enough to receive maximum benefit from the opportunities offered by the Craig Goch enlargement, the Kielder scheme on the North Tyne, or storage in the Dee estuary. Maximum benefit will come only if effective combinations of units can be formed.

Does the system encourage efficiency in water use and in public investment?

In theory, well-designed charging policies can induce a more efficient use of scarce resources and so reduce water service costs below the level they would otherwise have reached, but as yet there are few signs of this in practice. Charges for piped supplies and for direct abstractions have been fixed at levels sufficient to raise the revenue necessary to cover costs, but the structure of the charges – how they are distributed between different groups of consumers – has not been designed to influence the way water is used.

In chapter 4 we saw that abstraction charges are determined according to an abstraction's effect upon the resource – what remains in quality and quantity for other users. It happens that this results in high value uses such as domestic and industrial supply being charged less than lower value uses such as spray irrigation, but it can be argued that high value uses can afford to pay more for water and would use it less wastefully if charges were higher. Another criticism of abstraction charges from an efficiency point of view is that they are levied on licensed quantities and not on quantities of water actually taken. If an abstractor does economise on use, he gets no financial benefit unless his licence is revised downwards.

For piped water there is an important distinction between metered and unmetered supplies. With metered supplies, typically to industry, there is some incentive to reduce wasteful use, since charges are determined by the quantity of water drawn off. With unmetered supplies to houses and small commercial premises, there is no such incentive because charges are fixed according to the property's rateable value. Again, economy in use receives no financial reward.

It is unclear just what savings in consumption there might be if water meters were more widely used. If any case there is no possibility of early installation of meters in all existing houses, but domestic supplies in Malvern have been metered for some years, and new houses everywhere could be equipped with water meters without difficulty. In predicting the economic effects of metering, the meter and the charging tariff must be considered together, and the National Water Council (1976: appendix IV) has recommended additional metering and charging trials.

After use, water attracts no charge where it is returned direct to a river or the sea. Where it is put into the public sewers the charges levied reflect conveyance, treatment and disposal costs, calculated according to various formulae of volume, suspended load and biological load. Some of the more obvious pollution prevention costs are thus passed back to the dischargers, but those who discharge direct avoid pollution costs themselves and pass them on to society. Such a dissociation of benefits and costs must be counted as a disincentive to efficient operation.

Charges for abstracted and returned water *could* be applied in ways which would improve efficiency, and the Committee on Economic and Financial Policies in the Water Industry (Department of the Environment 1974b) considered at length the principles of efficient charging, in the hopes of encouraging movement in this direction. At present the main controls on the allocation of water services and administrative, not economic, and are likely to remain so until we have more detailed information about the sensitivity of demand for water services to the charges made for them. The immediate aim must be, as the Committee concluded: 'to ensure that, given the inadequacies of existing knowledge, the incentives point broadly in the right direction' (Department of the Environment 1974b: 42).

As for the balance between investment in water services and investment in other sectors of the economy, we find that the withdrawal of government subsidies from the water services has forced the water industry into financial independence. One form of subsidy remains, in grants from the Ministry of Agriculture, Fisheries and Food towards approved schemes for land drainage and flood prevention. This is a direct subsidy and one that is likely to be given for some years to come. However, schemes are approved only after economic appraisal of their worthwhileness in relation to their costs, and this guards against gross misallocation of funds.

Costs of all other water services must be met by the Water Authorities from funds raised from their consumers. While consumers are prepared to meet the bills, a Water Authority can devise any number of schemes for improving its services. When consumers reach their limit of tolerance and refuse to pay more, improvements stop. This is an excellent curb on excess expenditure by a Water Authority. Of course, certain levels of water services are essential and a Water Authority is a monopolistic supplier. To some extent, therefore, otherwise unacceptable charges can be imposed, but beyond these levels of service consumer control is reestablished and, assuming adequate representation within a Water Authority, consumers can influence the overall level of Water Authority expenditure and its division between the different water services.

A complication is introduced by the 'equalisation of charges' issue discussed in chapter 8. If regional variability is reduced by a redistribution of funds among the Authorities, charges no longer accurately reflect regional costs and the economic link between a consumer and his Water Authority is weakened. The scheme for partial equalisation contained in the Water Charges Equalisation Act 1977 attempts to preserve the consumer/Water Authority relationship in a direct and effective form, by allowing only that inter-Authority transfer of funds necessary to reduce the grosser inequalities due to historical accident.

Can all relevant interests contribute to water management decisions?

If the management system does not work automatically towards an efficient allocation of resources through its charging policies – and we have concluded above that it does not work in this way – then administrative allocation is necessary. This will be satisfactory only if decisions are based on a consideration of all the interests affected, with all interests having access to the decision-making body. Powerful lobbies of particular interests and the non-representation of others will lead to distortion and misallocation.

Everyone is a user of water services, and everyone is represented in a Water Authority by the local authority membership. Local authority members are in the majority on the governing board, and the *general* interests of all consumers seem adequately represented by this means. The special interests of particular groups, industrialists, spray irrigators, fishermen and so on, may also be conveyed through local authority members, some of whom may be closely involved with these groups. Another channel for representing particular interests is the specialist, Ministerially appointed membership. Clearly land drainage, flood prevention and fisheries are the special responsibility of members appointed by the Minister of Agriculture.

Less formal is the liaison between a Water Authority and outside bodies such as the Confederation of British Industry and the National Farmers' Union, representing major consumer groups. During the 1976 drought both these organisations strengthened their links with the Water Authorities to make sure their members' points of view were understood. Water restrictions on industry in south east Wales and on agriculture in East Anglia were worked out in detail with the consumer groups, so that the overall reduction required by the Water Authority was achieved with a minimum of disruption to economic activity.

Both Water Authority membership and local liaison arrangements were considered in the *Review* and are still under discussion, for strong objections have been raised to the present systems. Much of the discontent stems from the local authorities' loss of power in the reorganisation of water services. Where previously the separate local authorities looked after their own works for water supply and sewage treatment, now they may not be represented at all in their own right. For instance, sixty-six district councils nominate only nine members of the Anglian Water Authority and seventy-one metropolitan and non-metropolitan districts nominate eleven members of the Severn–Trent Water Authority. As a result some local authorities have no direct voice in Water Authority decisions. If this objection were to be met, the membership would increase enormously, probably to the detriment of efficient management. Instead of this, and to facilitate discussions with other interested bodies as well, the *Review* proposed that advisory committees be set up, to give permanent, statutory machinery for consultation.

No system of representation or consultation will perfectly reflect the balance of interests within a Water Authority area and do away with all conflict. Eventually someone will find a particular Water Authority decision unacceptable and will wish to make this known in the hopes of effecting a revision. Craine (1969), in his study of the Water Resources Act 1963, noted the detailed provisions for hearings and appeals against determinations of minimum acceptable flow and against abstraction licensing and charging schemes, these giving protection against arbitrary and capricious action and assuring every party of interest a chance to be heard. The more recent legislation seems to favour a non-appellate system. For example, on the very important issue of charges for water services, section 31(4) of the Water Act 1973 demands that 'All charges schemes shall be so framed as to show the methods by which and the principles on which the charges are to be made, and shall be published in such a manner as in the opinion of the authority will secure adequate publicity for them' but there are no provisions for appeal. As water abstractors have come to appreciate this change, many of them have asked the Water Authorities just how and when they should make representations on matters of licensing and charging. No doubt rather different answers have been given by the different Authorities, but the statutory advisory committees, if established, may help to reduce the ambiguity of the present arrangements.

Are there effective links between management units, with national bodies and with central government?

Chapter 8 has shown that despite the essentially regional organisation of the water industry, there are substantial issues to be decided at inter-regional or national level. Predominantly self-sufficient in water resources, the Water Authorities still rely on inter-regional water transfers for some of the big cities which, at the end of the last century, 'took to the distant hills' for their water supply. Inter-regional transfers of funds are at present quite small, associated with the operation and maintenance costs of works for water transfer, but we have a new equalisation scheme to reduce some of the regional variation in water service changes and have seen suggestions for premiums on water exported from Wales. The acute local water shortages suffered during 1976 rekindled interest in the idea of a water grid, and future plans for source development and distribution are sure to contain elements of inter-regional transfer as well as of within-region provision.

Some of these physical and financial transfers can be decided simply through good working relations between two particular Water Authorities. No special arrangements are necessary to involve other parties. But increasingly it is appreciated that the use of water in one way precludes its use in other ways. The use of a reservoir for river and aqueduct transfer to an adjacent Water Authority, while agreeable to both the exporting and the importing Authorities, may not be the best from a national point of view if it rules out an alternative and more productive scheme to serve a different or a larger region. A good, overall national strategy will not necessarily emerge from individual inter-Authority agreements.

The Water Authorities operate under the guidance of the central government, which imposes strict controls on capital expenditure and gives more gentle assistance on techniques and assumptions for planning. The Water Act 1973 polarised responsibilities for water, with Ministers on one side and the regional units on the other, clearing away the Water Resources Board which was previously interposed between them. The National Water Council, in some senses the Board's replacement, is far less of an obstacle to communication between Westminster and the regional units, since it is primarily the Water Authorities in council, without a large policy-making machinery of its own.

The present links between the individual Water Authorities, with the National Water Council and with the central government are well-defined. A Water Authority may negotiate and conclude an agreement with any other Water Authority, and the National Water Council, of which its chairman is a member, provides it with a forum for discussion with all the Authorities together. Water Authority plans for capital works must be submitted to Ministers for approval, and Ministers may, when they consider it necessary, direct a Water Authority to modify its plans.

Why, then, is it proposed to change these arrangements by putting a new body, the National Water Authority, between Westminster and the regions? National issues in water management have grown in importance since the Water Act first took shape, and the creation of a new Ministerial responsibility for water resources during the 1976 drought gave this an exceptional emphasis. There can be no question that a national organisation is needed to coordinate and supervise the work of the regions, but the Ministers already have this responsibility and their own staffs to help them discharge it.

One of the aims is to draw together water research, development planning and policy formulation, activities presently divided between the Water Research Centre, the Central Water Planning Unit and the National Water Council. For these activities are at the very least complementary if not inseparable, and their apportionment to self-contained units raises innumerable problems for coordinating work and avoiding duplication. In a single, larger organisation such problems do not evaporate altogether, but the chances of effective work planning seem greater.

Another aim is to produce a national strategy for the water services. While there is agreement that certain matters must be considered nationally, there is disagreement on what exactly these matters are and on whether their consideration should be solely a Ministerial or also a sub-Ministerial responsibility. In favour of the proposals set out in the *Review* is the easier access this could give to the policy-making body. The individual Water Authorities, the users of water services and the non-water interests affected by water development schemes, meeting together in an organisation independent of central government, would be better placed for a free discussion and might well be able to defuse potential conflicts which, if allowed to grow into submissions to a Minister, would become too formalised for amicable resolution.

Conclusions

The Water Act 1973 was no minor adjustment of responsibilities but a fundamental and far-reaching management change. Maybe it was not intended as a Water Act to end Water Acts, but certainly one might have expected it to be followed by a period of legislative stability in which the Water Authorities and the National Water Council could grow into their new roles. In place of stability, there is continuing change.

The government's review of the water industry, conducted while the industry was still finding its feet after reorganisation, confirmed some of the new arrangements but proposed major changes in others. The local authorities are dissatisfied with their representation in the Water Authorities and have pressed for changes in the membership. Increased charges for water services have given rise to suggestions of surcharges, equalisation schemes and extended use of water meters. Devolution proposals for Wales have emphasised a boundary problem in that the Principality and the Welsh National Water Development Authority are not coextensive, and the 1976 drought, producing a new Minister and an *ad hoc* Emergency Water Committee, suggests that the permanent organisation at national level is deficient in a crisis.

To recapitulate on our six criteria, it seems that the Water Authorities have all the management powers they need and that their areas of jurisdiction are reasonable. The water companies have still to be fully integrated with the Water Authorities, but only comparatively small adjustments are needed to effect this. Based on large river basins or groups of basins, the Authorities are able to manage water 'from source to the sea', and the boundaries as presently drawn unite source and consumer in all but a few cases. Water Authorities founded on hydrology do not necessarily correspond to any other administrative areas, giving particular complications in the Welsh Borders but, if the river basin principle is to be maintained, one must bear with such inevitabilities and seek to minimise them through the system of representation.

A management power available to the Water Authorities but yet to be used to maximum effect is the power to levy charges for water services. In general the charges levied cover costs, since most forms of government subsidy to the water industry have been withdrawn, but the way the charges fall on individual users is, more often than not, little encouragement to efficiency in use. Here one might expect considerable changes in the future. If charges are further increased to finance improved water services and to reduce the industry's excessive borrowing requirement, consumers may well press for greater control over their water service bills, insisting that, wherever possible, charges be levied on the quantities of water drawn off or effluent taken away. The Water Authorities are likely to welcome this, provided that metered systems induce economies in use sufficient to offset the additional costs.

The representation of relevant interests within the regional unit is still a matter of controversy, especially with the local authorities. Possible changes ahead include the alteration of Water Authority membership and the establishment of statutory advisory committees to improve access for those interests not directly represented on the boards.

But it is the issue of national coordination that is the most contentious. The government has veered first one way and then another over the desirability of a strong and independent national water organisation, reflecting deep differences of opinion. Its proposals for a National Water Authority have been criticised on the grounds that the new organisation will 'blur responsibilities, and add to delays', since decisions that cannot be taken by the Water Authorities themselves can only be taken by Ministers (Zuckerman and Chilver 1976). The author is more hopeful that a National Water Authority would increase the chances of agreement between different water interests and that the national plans eventually endorsed by Ministers would have a wider acceptability.

Perhaps the next round of water management legislation will bring the stability denied the industry after the Water Act 1973. In some sense stability and change go together, for appropriate and long-enduring legislation is that which gives flexibility to its institutions. Rainfall patterns, demands for water services, and groupings of affected interests are all liable to change, and the management system must be able to adjust both its operating techniques and its representation of affected interests to accommodate them. The Water Authorities enjoy a very high degree of flexibility in their physical operations, thanks to the 1973 Act. Now one looks to a second phase of reorganisation to resolve representation problems and to provide a useful, flexible and enduring national organisation.

REFERENCES

Note: the place of publication is omitted for books published in the United Kingdom.

Advisory Committee on Water 1925 *Report on Measures for the Protection of Underground Water*. Ministry of Health.

Arvill, R. 1967 *Man and Environment*.

Boulton, A. G. 1965 'Minimum acceptable flow'. *Journal of the Institute of Water Engineers* **19**, 15–31.

Briggs, A. 1968 *Victorian Cities*.

Bugler, J. 1972 *Polluting Britain*.

Central Advisory Water Committee 1938 First report. *Underground Water*; *Planning of Water Resources and Supplies*. Ministry of Health.

1943 Third report. *River Boards*. Ministry of Health. Cmd 6465.

1960 Sub-Committee on the Growing Demand for Water. Second report.

1963 Report of the Sub-Committee on Water Charges. Ministry of Housing and Local Government.

1971 *The Future Management of Water in England and Wales*. Department of the Environment.

Chadwick, M. J., Edworthy, K. J., Rush, D. and Williams, P. J. 1974 'Ecosystem irrigation as a means of groundwater recharge and water quality improvement'. *Journal of Applied Ecology* **11**, 231–47.

Chorley, R. J. and More, R. J. 1969 'The interaction of precipitation and man'. In *Water, Earth and Man*, ed. R. J. Chorley, 157–66.

Clutterbuck, J. J. 1850 'On the periodical alternations and progressive permanent depression of the Chalk water levels under London'. *Proceedings of the Institution of Civil Engineers* **9**, 151–5.

Conservators of the River Thames 1936 Resolution dated June 1936.

Craine, L. E. 1969 *Water Management Innovations in England*. The Johns Hopkins Press, Baltimore.

Day, H. J. 1973 *Benefit and Cost Analysis of Hydrological Forecasts*. World Meteorological Organization. Operational Hydrology Report 3. Geneva.

Department of the Environment 1972 *Out of Sight, Out of Mind*. Report of a working party on sludge disposal in Liverpool Bay.

1973a *The New Water Industry: Management and Structure*. Report of the Management Structure Committee.

1973b *The Water Services: Economic and Financial Policies*. First report to the Secretary of State for the Environment.

1974a *The Water Services: Economic and Financial Policies*. Second report to the Secretary of State for the Environment.

1974b *The Water Services: Economic and Financial Policies*. Third report to the Secretary of State for the Environment.

Department of the Environment and Welsh Office 1970 *Taken for Granted*. Report of the working party on sewage disposal.

1971 *Report of a River Pollution Survey of England and Wales 1970*.

Department of the Environment, Welsh Office and Ministry of Agriculture, Fisheries and Food 1976 *Review of the Water Industry in England and Wales*.

Dolbey, S. J. 1974 'The politics of Manchester's water supply 1961–7'. In *Campaigning for the Environment*, ed. R. Kimber and J. J. Richardson, 75–102.

Fox, I. K. 1966 'Policy problems in the field of water resources'. In *Water Research*, ed. A. V. Kneese and S. C. Smith, 271–89. The Johns Hopkins Press, Baltimore.

Goddard, J. E. 1961 'The cooperative program in the Tennessee Valley'. In *Papers on Flood Problems*, ed. G. F. White. University of Chicago, Department of Geography Research Paper **70**, 148–68. Chicago.

Great Ouse Groundwater Pilot Scheme 1971 *Third Progress Report for 1970*.

1972a *Fourth Progress Report for 1971*.

1972b *Steering Committee Final Report*.

Great Ouse River Authority 1973 *Eighth Annual Report 1972–3*.

1974 'Periodic survey of the water resources and future demand within the Great Ouse River Authority'. In draft.

Grinsted, W. A. 1974 'The measurement of areal rainfall by the use of radar'. In *Environmental Remote Sensing: Applications and Achievements*, ed. E. C. Barrett and L. F. Curtis, 269–83.

Hall, W. A. and Dracup, J. A. 1970 *Water Resources Systems Engineering*. McGraw-Hill, New York.

Harding, D. M. and Parker, D. J. 1974 'Flood hazard at Shrewsbury, United Kingdom'. In *Natural Hazards: Global, National, Local*, ed. G. F. White, 45–52.

Harding, D. M. and Porter, E. 1970 'Flood loss information and economic aspects of flood plain occupance'. *Proceedings of the Institution of Civil Engineers* **46**, 403–9.

Harwood, Sir John J. 1895 *History and Description of the Thirlmere Water Scheme*.

HMSO 1975 *Our Changing Democracy: Devolution to Scotland and Wales*. Cmd 6348.

Hollis, G. E. 1974 'River management and urban flooding'. In *Conservation in Practice*, ed. A. Warren and F. B. Goldsmith, 201–16.

Institution of Civil Engineers 1967 *Flood Studies for the United Kingdom*. Report of the Committee on Floods in the United Kingdom.

Jackson, C. I. 1969 Preface to J. A. Rees' *Industrial Demand for Water: a Study of South-east England*.

Jamieson, D. G. 1972 'River Dee Research Program: operating multi-purpose reservoir systems for water supply and flood alleviation'. *Water Resources Research* **8** no 4, 899–903. American Geophysical Union, Washington DC.

Johnson, E. A. G. 1966 'Land drainage in England and Wales'. In *River Engineering and Water Conservation Works*, ed. R. B. Thorn, 29–46.

1973 'Current potential for economic studies'. *Proceedings of a Symposium on Floods*, Middlesex Polytechnic, 8 May 1973, 1–3.

Klein, L. 1957 *Aspects of River Pollution*. Academic Press, Inc., New York.

Lee Conservancy Catchment Board 1973 *Proposed Scheme of Artificial Recharge in the Lower Lee Valley*. Engineer's report.

Lester, W. F., Woodward, G. M. and Raven, T. W. 1972 'The effect and cost of river purification lakes'. *Institute of Water Pollution Control Symposium*, Nottingham.

Lindblom, C. E. 1959 'The science of "muddling through"'. *Public Administration Review* **19** no 2, 79–88. Washington DC.

Mackay, D. M. and Topping, G. 1970 'Preliminary report on the effects of sludge disposal at sea. *Effluent and Water Treatment Journal* **5**, 641–9.

Manchester Corporation Waterworks 1969 *Ullswater/Windermere Scheme: Ullswater Works*.

1974a *Water for the Millions*.

1974b *Chronology: 1847–1974*.

Marshall, H. 1964 'Rational choice in water resources planning'. In *Economics and Public Policy in Water Resource Development*, ed. S. C. Smith and E. N. Castle, 403–23. Iowa State University Press.

Marsland, A. 1966 'The design and construction of earthen floodbanks'. In *River Engineering and Water Conservation Works*, ed. R. B. Thorn, 361–92.

Mersey and Weaver River Authority 1970 'General review of pollution in the area of the Authority'. Unpublished paper.

Ministry of Agriculture, Fisheries and Food 1954 *The Calculation of Irrigation Need*. Technical Bulletin **4**.

1974 Memorandum. 'Guidance notes for Water Authorities: Water Act 1973, section 24 surveys'.

Ministry of Housing and Local Government 1960 *Great Ouse River Basin: Hydrological Survey*.

1965 *Report on the Water Resources of the Great Ouse Basin*. Binnie and Partners.

1966 Memorandum. 'Technical problems of River Authorities and Sewage Disposal Authorities in laying down and complying with limits of quality for effluents more restrictive than those of the Royal Commission'.

1967 *Dee Crossing Study: Phase 1*.

Ministry of Housing and Local Government and Ministry of Agriculture, Fisheries and Food 1962 Joint circular **52/62**. 'Liaison between planning authorities and River Boards'.

Ministry of Housing and Local Government and Welsh Office 1967 'Memorandum of advice on the preparation of charging schemes under section 58 of the Water Resources Act 1963'.

1969 Circulars **94/69** and **97/69**. 'Surface water run-off from development'.

Ministry of Town and Country Planning 1947 Circular **31**. 'Liaison between planning authorities and land drainage authorities'.

National Water Council 1975a *First Annual Report and Accounts 1974–5*.

1975b *Views of the National Water Council on the Water Resources Board Report 'Water Resources in England and Wales'*.

1976 *Paying for Water*.

1977 *The 1975–76 Drought*.

Natural Environment Research Council 1975 *Flood Studies Report*.

Nixon, M. 1963 'Flood regulation and river training in England and Wales'. *Institution of Civil Engineers' Symposium on the Conservation of Water Resources in the United Kingdom*, 137–50.

North West Water Authority 1975 *First Annual Report 1974–5*.

Office of the Minister of Science 1962 *Irrigation in Great Britain*. Report of the Natural Resources (Technical) Committee.

O'Riordan, T. 1970 'Spray irrigation and the Water Resources Act 1963'. *Institute of British Geographers Transactions* **49**, 33–47.

1971 *Perspectives on Resource Management*.

O'Riordan, T. and More R. J. 1969 'Choice in water use'. In *Water, Earth and Man*, ed. R. J. Chorley, 547–73.

Parker, D. J. and Chatterton, J. B. 1974 'The development of flood damage information: a preliminary analysis'. Paper presented at the Conference of River Engineers, Cranfield.

Peak Park Planning Board 1971 *A New Look at Water Resources: an Examination of* the Feasibility of Securing Water Resources other than by the Creation of Storage Reservoirs.

Penman, H. L. 1948 'Natural evaporation from open water, bare soil and grass'. *Proceedings of the Royal Society (London) Series A* **193**, 120–45.

Penning-Rowsell, E. C. and Chatterton, J. B. 1977 *The Benefits of Flood Alleviation: A Manual of Assessment Techniques.*

Penning-Rowsell, E. C. and Parker, D. J. 1974 'Improving flood plain development control'. *Journal of the Royal Town Planning Institute* **60** no 2, 540–3.

The Policy-holder 1961 Editorial, 10 August 1961, 1066–7.

Porter, E. 1971 'Assessing flood damage'. *Spectrum: British Science News* **84**, 2–5.

1973 *Pollution in Four Industrialised Estuaries* HMSO.

Prickett, C. N. 1966 'Water supply and conservation for agriculture'. In *River Engineering and Water Conservation Works*, ed. R. B. Thorn, 441–78.

Roberts, D. B. 1973 'Flood alleviation – problems in choosing a design standard'. *Proceedings of a Symposium on Economic Aspects of Floods*. Middlesex Polytechnic, 8 May 1973, 40–5.

Royal Commission on Environmental Pollution 1972 Third report. *Pollution in some British Estuaries and Coastal Waters*. Cmd 5054.

Royal Commission on Sewage Disposal 1912 Eighth report. *Standards and Tests for Sewage and Sewage Effluents Discharging into Rivers and Streams*. Cd 6464.

Royal Commission on Water Supply 1869 'Report of the Commissioners on the means of obtaining additional supplies of unpolluted and wholesome water for the Metropolis and other large towns'.

Russell, C. S. 1974 'Restraining demand'. In *The Management of Water Resources in England and Wales*, ed. B. M. Funnell and R. D. Hey, 90–8.

Rydz, B. 1974 'Water needs and resources'. In *The Management of Water Resources in England and Wales*, ed. B. M. Funnell and R. D. Hey, 1–8.

Secretary of State for the Environment 1971 House of Commons, 2 December 1971.

Severn–Trent Water Authority 1974a 'River Idle: improved drainage of the lower reach'.

1974b *Water Quality 1973.*

Sewell, W. R. D. and Bower, B. T. 1968 *Forecasting the Demands for Water*. Department of Energy, Mines and Resources, Ottawa.

Simon, H. A. 1960 *Administrative Behavior*. Second edition. Macmillan, New York.

1967 'Theories of decision-making in economics and behavioural science'. In *Surveys of Economic Theory – Volume III – Resource Allocation*. American Economic Association and Royal Economic Society, 1–28.

Smith, C. T. 1969 'The drainage basin as an historical basis for human activity'. In *Water, Earth and Man*, ed. R. J. Chorley, 107–9.

Smith, K. 1972 *Water in Britain.*

Sterland, F. K. and Nixon, M. 1972 'Flood plain regulation in the United Kingdom'. *International Commission on Drainage and Irrigation, Eighth Congress, session* 29.2, 27–46 Varna.

Tatham, W. 1801 *National Irrigation or the Various Methods of Watering Meadows; Affording Means to Increase the Population, Wealth, and Revenue of the Kingdom, by an Agricultural, Commercial and General Economy in the Use of Water.*

Thames Conservancy 1972 'Report on the Lambourn Valley Pilot Scheme 1967–9'.

Toplis, F. 1879 'Suggestions for dividing England and Wales into watershed districts'. *Journal of the Society of Arts* **27** 696–709.

Trent River Authority 1970 'Flood forecasting and flood warning procedure'.

1972 'The work of the Pollution Control and Fisheries Department'.

Trent River Board 1962 'Supplementary report on the River Leen Improvement Scheme: detailed investigation into the flooding of the Meadows Area'.

1963 'Supplementary report on the River Leen Improvement Scheme: investigation into the River Leen catchment upstream of the Meadows Area'.

United States Army, Office of the Chief of Engineers 1972 *Flood-Proofing Regulations*. Washington DC.

United States Federal Committee for Science and Technology 1971 *A National Program for Accelerating Progress in Weather Modification*. Interdepartmental Committee on Atmospheric Sciences, report **15a**. Washington DC.

University of Hull/Humber Advisory Group 1974 *The Humber Estuary* Proceedings of a joint symposium, 12 and 13 December 1973.

van Oosterom, H., Downing, R. A. and Law, F. M. 1973 'Development of the Chalk aquifer in the Great Ouse Basin'. Institution of Civil Engineers, Hydrological Group Informal Discussion, 8 January 1973.

Walford, C. 1876 *The Insurance Cyclopaedia* **4**.

Water Power Resources Committee 1920 Second interim report. Board of Trade. Cmd 776.

Water Resources Board 1966a *Water Supplies in South East England*.

1966b *Morecambe and Solway Barrages: Report on Desk Studies*.

1969 *Report on Desalination for England and Wales*.

1970 *Water Resources in the North*.

1971 *Water Resources in Wales and the Midlands*.

1972a *Artificial Recharge of the London Basin: Hydrogeology*.

1972b *The Hydrogeology of the London Basin*.

1972c *Artificial Recharge: Bunter Sandstone*. The Trent Research Programme **7**.

1972d *The Economic Model*. The Trent Research Programme **11**.

1972e *River Purification Lakes*. The Trent Research Programme **6**.

1972f *Desalination 1972*.

1973a *Water Resources in England and Wales*.

1973b *Artificial Recharge of the London Basin: Electrical Analogue Model Studies*.

1974 *Evaluation of the Economic Model*. The Trent Research Programme **12**.

Water Resources Board, Meteorological Office and Plessey Radar Ltd 1973 *The Use of a Radar Network for the Measurement and Quantitative Forecasting of Precipitation*.

Watson, J. D. and Watson, D. M. 1968 *Tees-side Sewerage and Sewage Disposal*. Final report.

1974 *Merseyside Sewerage and Sewage Disposal*.

Welsh Office 1975 'Report of the Committee of Inquiry into water charges in the area of the Welsh National Water Development Authority'.

Wisdom, A. S. 1962 *The Law of Rivers and Water Courses*.

1966 *The Law on the Pollution of Waters*. Second edition.

Withers, W. B. J. 1973 'The evolution and evaluation of irrigation in Britain'. *The Agricultural Engineer*, Winter 1973, 136–9.

Wollman, N. 1962 *The Value of Water in Alternative Uses*. University of New Mexico Press, Albuquerque.

Woodward, G. M. 1975 'Pollution detection and river quality management'. *Water Treatment and Examination* **24**, 3–20.

Zuckerman, S. and Chilver, R. C. 1976 Letter to *The Times*, published 8 September 1976.

LEGISLATION CITED

Clean Rivers (Estuaries and Tidal Waters) Act 1960 8 & 9 Eliz 2 ch 54.
Control of Pollution Act 1974 ch 40.
Drought Act 1976 ch 44.
Land Drainage Act 1930 20 & 21 Geo 5 ch 44.
Land Drainage Act 1961 9 & 10 Eliz 2 ch 48.
Land Drainage (Amendment) Act 1976 ch 17.
Public Health Act 1875 38 & 39 Vict ch 55.
Public Health Act 1936 26 Geo 5 & 1 Edw 8 ch 49.
River Boards Act 1948 11 & 12 Geo 6 ch 32.
Rivers Pollution Prevention Act 1876 39 & 40 Vict ch 75.
Rivers (Prevention of Pollution) Act 1951 14 & 15 Geo 6 ch 64.
Rivers (Prevention of Pollution) Act 1961 9 & 10 Eliz 2 ch 50.
Town and Country Planning Act 1962 10 & 11 Eliz 2 ch 38.
Water Act 1945 8 & 9 Geo 6 ch 42.
Water Act 1973 ch 37.
Water Charges Equalisation Act 1977 ch 41.
Water Resources Act 1963 ch 38.
Water Resources Act 1971 ch 34.
Waterworks Clauses Act 1847 10 & 11 Vict ch 17.
Waterworks Clauses Act 1863 26 & 27 Vict ch 93.

INDEX